Julius Caesar

JULIUS CAESAR

A Guide to the Play

JO MCMURTRY

Greenwood Guides to Shakespeare

Greenwood Press
Westport, Connecticut • London

Library of Congress Cataloging-in-Publication Data

McMurtry, Jo.
    Julius Caesar : a guide to the play / Jo McMurtry
       p.   cm. — (Greenwood guides to Shakespeare)
    Includes bibliographical references and index.
    ISBN 0–313–30479–3 (alk. paper)
    1. Shakespeare, William, 1564–1616. Julius Caesar. 2. Caesar,
Julius—In literature. 3. Rome—In literature. 4. Tragedy.
    I. Title. II. Series.
    PR2808.M38   1998
    822.3′3—dc21   98–15598

British Library Cataloguing in Publication Data is available.

Library of Congress Catalog Card Number: 98–15598
ISBN: 0–313–30479–3

First published in 1998

Greenwood Press, 88 Post Road West, Westport, CT 06881
An imprint of Greenwood Publishing Group, Inc.

Printed in the United States of America

The paper used in this book complies with the
Permanent Paper Standard issued by the National
Information Standards Organization (Z39.48–1984).

10 9 8 7 6 5 4 3 2 1

CONTENTS

PREFACE

Julius Caesar: A Guide to the Play is a reference book intended for both long-time Shakespeareans and those who are coming to *Julius Caesar*, and perhaps to Shakespeare as well, for the first time. *Julius Caesar* has so often served as an introduction to Shakespeare that the probability of a substantial group of readers belonging to the second category would seem comparatively high. Consequently, I have tried to make few assumptions about readers' prior knowledge, and I have included signposts to scholarly and critical works readers may wish to consult in order to fill in bits of background. I have resisted the urge to get into lengthy comparisons of *Julius Caesar* with any of Shakespeare's other plays. This kind of excursion can be delightful if one knows both the works under discussion, but deadening if one does not.

For the same reason, I have not emphasized analytical approaches that cannot easily be understood unless the reader has a general grasp of all Shakespeare's plays—all the tragedies, all the Roman dramas, or any other category of previous detailed experience; and I have not cited at length critical works that discuss *Julius Caesar* but seem to mention two or three other plays in every sentence. (I have listed some of these works in the annotated bibliography, however.) The focus here is on *Julius Caesar*.

Julius Caesar: A Guide to the Play is organized so that its chapters may be read independently of one another. Readers may start at any point, guided perhaps by the contents or the index. Since many passages in this play lend themselves to analysis from many angles, the reader moving from one chapter to another may experience a certain sense of déjà vu. I have tried to vary the examples as much as possible, but from time to time the same lines do recur.

Chapter 1, "Textual History," discusses the text of *Julius Caesar*, a simple matter in comparison to some of Shakespeare's other plays. In addition, this chapter goes into the development of Shakespearean reading texts since the seventeenth century, answering some of the questions my students have asked when they notice that the text they are reading looks very different from facsimile pages of the earliest editions—the First Folio of 1623, for example, in which *Julius Caesar* was originally published. A description of currently available editions of *Julius Caesar* is included at the end of the chapter.

Chapter 2, "Contexts and Sources," concerns itself with the world of Shakespeare and his audience, especially the audience of 1599, when *Julius Caesar* was first acted at the Globe Theatre. This audience, or members of the audience who read and bought books, had access to Shakespeare's main source, Thomas North's version of Plutarch's *Lives of the Noble Grecians and Romans*. Those who had read it would have been especially alert as they watched—or, as the Elizabethans often said, "heard"—the play.

In Chapter 3, "Dramatic Structure," we go inside the play to focus on the five-act structure, the development of the characters, stylistic variations such as the use of prose and verse, and the importance of rhetoric—the art of persuasion—in this drama composed so frequently of public speeches.

Chapter 4, "Themes," considers the large-scale and universal ideas found in this play, with special attention to the image patterns that support and emphasize these ideas. The nature of the topic implies a great deal of close attention to individual words and phrases.

Chapter 5, "Critical Approaches," is concerned largely with recent critical work—that done within the past thirty years or so. This is not the result of chronological snobbery but of the fact that recent criticism has particularly tended to relate Shakespeare's works to ideas found outside the field of literary study—to philosophy, sociology, and economics, to mention only a few. Discussing these approaches, in general or as applied to *Julius Caesar*, requires a special context, which this chapter supplies. I might add that scholarly and critical works are, of course, cited throughout this book, whenever they are relevant to the topic at hand.

Chapter 6, "The Play in Performance," surveys four hundred years of stage activity, naturally from a very selective basis. Attention is also given to films, especially to those that are readily available on videotape or video laserdisc.

I cannot claim total objectivity in my role as guide, but I have tried to present ideas and interpretations as optional rather than compulsory choices. To say the last word on any aspect of Shakespeare's work is not in the realm of reality, and I hope I have not given the impression that it is.

Quotations from *Julius Caesar* are taken from the second edition (1997) of the *Riverside Shakespeare,* edited by G. Blakemore Evans. Sources of other quotations are cited in the notes.

I am grateful to many people for helping to make this book possible. First in line are my students, whose alert and curious minds make our joint explorations of Shakespeare a continuing delight. David Leary, dean of arts and sciences at the University of Richmond, and Ray Hilliard, chair of the English Department, were instrumental in my receiving a sabbatical leave for the autumn of 1997. The university's Faculty Research Committee, chaired by Philip Rubin, gave me a much-appreciated grant for research expenses. Nancy Vick and Betty Dickie in the

University of Richmond library respectively found interlibrary loan books for me and rescued me from predatory microfilm machines. Among the University of Richmond's computer wizards I am grateful to Cely Coleman, Laurel Moore, and a host of student assistants.

I have received much help from the staff of the Folger Shakespeare Library, Jean Miller in particular. Abroad, the staff of the British Library was unfailingly efficient and courteous to its readers, despite the complexities of the then-forthcoming move to the new building at St. Pancras. I especially appreciate the time spent on my project by Nina Jacob, of the reconstructed Shakespeare's Globe in London, and Sylvia Morris, of the Shakespeare Centre Library at Stratford-upon-Avon. For *Julius Caesar*–centered conversations, bibliographies, and background material, I am grateful to Dan Bartges, Mike Evans, and Anthony Russell.

I have been greatly helped by my editors at Greenwood Press: George F. Butler, acquisitions editor; Rebecca Ardwin, production editor; and Beverly Miller, copy-editor. They have pointed my way, answered my questions, and rescued me from errors, ambiguities, and general infelicities. Any follies remaining are entirely my own.

ABBREVIATIONS OF CITED WORKS

AI	*American Imago*
CompD	*Comparative Drama*
ELH	*English Literary History*
ELN	*English Language Notes*
ELR	*English Literary Renaissance*
JEGP	*Journal of English and Germanic Philology*
L&P	*Literature and Psychology*
LFQ	*Literature/Film Quarterly*
MLN	*Modern Language Notes*
MLR	*Modern Language Review*
PMLA	*Publications of the Modern Language Association*
PQ	*Philological Quarterly*
RenD	*Renaissance Drama*
RenQ	*Renaissance Quarterly*
SEL	*Studies in English Literature*
SFNL	*Shakespeare on Film Newsletter*
ShB	*Shakespeare Bulletin*
ShN	*Shakespeare Newsletter*
ShS	*Shakespeare Survey*
ShStud	*Shakespeare Studies*
SP	*Studies in Philology*
SQ	*Shakespeare Quarterly*
TLS	*Times Literary Supplement* (London)

1

TEXTUAL HISTORY

THE AUTHORITATIVE TEXT: THE FIRST FOLIO

The single authoritative text of *Julius Caesar* is that of the First Folio of Shakespeare's plays, published in 1623. There are no other early editions. Unlike many of Shakespeare's other plays, *Julius Caesar* has no pre-1623 quarto edition, so scholars have no opportunity to be puzzled by variant texts. (*King Lear*, to mention only one contrasting example, was published in a quarto version so different from the later First Folio text that comparing the two has become something of a Shakespearean industry in itself.)

The First Folio, a large and impressive book containing all of the plays traditionally accepted as Shakespeare's except *Pericles* and *The Two Noble Kinsmen*, was put together seven years after the author's death by John Heminges and Henry Condell, two of Shakespeare's former associates at the Globe Theatre. It is generally assumed that these men would have had the judgment to know a good text from a bad one or, at any rate, a better text from a worse one, from the standpoint of what Shakespeare actually wrote, and would have used the best copies of the individual plays that they could obtain.

In the case of *Julius Caesar*, the text seems to have been very good indeed. Scholars speculate that it may have been used as a prompt copy, held by an assistant during rehearsals and used to prompt any actor who had not quite mastered his lines.[1] A prompt copy included all the parts and thus differed from an individual actor's copy, a considerably smaller sheaf of hand-written papers, typically consisting only of his own lines and the cues immediately preceding them. There are, of course, a few perplexities inherent in the text, but these are minor. Their non-world-shaking quality will in fact serve to demonstrate the dependability of the First Folio's *Julius Caesar* as a whole.

The names of the characters may vary in spelling from one modern edition to another. Murellus, one of the tribunes who appears in the opening scene, is often spelled "Marullus" by modern editors. The latter spelling occurs in Plutarch, Shakespeare's major source; presumably Shakespeare wrote the name as he remembered it. Or the variation could have originated with a scribe who copied Shakespeare's manuscript. Other variations in the names of minor characters include Caska, Calphurnia, Varrus, and Claudio, as spelled in the First Folio; editors may emend to Casca, Calpurnia, Varro, and Claudius, as these names appear in other historical sources. Some discrepancies occur within the First Folio. "Antony," as this character is spelled in *Julius Caesar*, appears as "Anthony" in *Antony and Cleopatra*. (The First Folio in fact prints this title as *The Tragedie of Anthonie, and Cleopatra*. Plutarch uses the spelling "Antonius.") Scholars have suggested that "Antony" in *Julius Caesar* was simply the preference of a scribe who at some point copied the manuscript.[2]

None of these variations is likely to puzzle readers, because modern editors simply make a choice and stick to it. Readers are similarly unaware of the few obvious misprints in the First Folio, since editors silently correct them. Brutus, for example, in the First Folio asks his servant Lucius, "Is not tomorrow, boy, the first of March?" (II.i.40). This line, which makes perfect sense in itself, nevertheless makes no sense in the time pattern of the play, since Brutus asks this question on the night (March 14) before Caesar is assassinated. Consequently the line is customarily changed to, "Is not tomorrow, boy, the Ides of March?" The error may have been made by a scribe or a typesetter, perhaps working from a scribbly manuscript or in poor light.

One line in the First Folio's *Julius Caesar* has no speech prefix: "And I am Brutus, Marcus Brutus, I," runs the line, in the midst of the battle of Philippi, unattributed to any of the characters (V.iv.7). Since, according to the First Folio, Brutus is on stage at the time, it would seem reasonable to assign the line to him. However, in the context of the scene, this solution does not work. Lucillius is here pretending to be Brutus, so he gets the line. Most editors also add an exit for Brutus just before Lucillius's pretense begins.

A textual matter that has given rise to considerable scholarly discussion is so abstruse as not even to exist in the First Folio as we have it; the discrepancy is based on conjecture. It can serve us here as an example of how curiously scholars are willing to consider. Ben Jonson, one of Shakespeare's fellow playwrights, wrote snippily about his competitor's nonsensical lines, citing as an example, "Caesar did never wrong, but with just cause."[3] On the assumption that Jonson was quoting correctly—that he made the criticism before the First Folio was published, and that Shakespeare's company heard of it and decided to change the line—scholars assume that the text as we have it represents an emendment: "Know, Caesar doth not wrong, nor without cause / Will he be satisfied" (III.i.47–48). Some readers find the conjectured original reading more satisfactory, pointing as it does to a pattern of self-contradiction in Caesar's personality. Trevor Nunn, directing a production of *Julius Caesar* in 1972, put Jonson's version into his script. "I'm sure that's the original. If one does take that to be the line, it's the ultimate statement of the power-obsessed dictator."[4]

Another textual tangle is visible even to casual readers and may well cause perplexity. During the quarrel between Brutus and Cassius, after the conspirators have fled from Rome, Brutus mentions rather casually that his wife, Portia, has killed herself by swallowing fire (IV.iii.147, 152–57). Cassius is horrified, offers his sympathy, and berates himself for having quarreled with his friend at such a time. A few minutes later, Messala enters with letters from Rome. He carefully prepares Brutus for bad news. When he asks Brutus if he has had any letters from or about Portia, Brutus says he has not. On Messala's "For certain she is dead, and by strange manner," Brutus replies:

> Why, farewell, Portia. We must die, Messala.
> With meditating that she must die once,
> I have the patience to endure it now.   (190–192)

Some scholars assume that Shakespeare wrote the first part of the scene, in which Brutus tells Cassius of Portia's death, but then changed his mind and instead made Messala the bearer of these tidings. Shakespeare then forgot to go back and cancel the earlier lines. Alternatively, other scholars claim that the correction is the other way round, that Shakespeare meant to cancel the dialogue with Messala.[5]

Either of these suggestions is possible. However, it is also possible that Shakespeare intended the duplication. Much evidence within the play, perceived with particular zeal by irony-conscious present-day readers, points to Brutus as a person greatly concerned with maintaining an outward image of nobility. Such a Brutus would have been quite capable of giving a set speech to Messala, carefully prepared in advance, while pretending to react with proper Stoic self-discipline to news he was apparently hearing for the first time. Certainly the effect of his calm reaction is to inspire his listeners with awe. "Even so great men great losses should endure," says Messala.

Cassius, in this passage, provides something of a stumbling block to the argument that Shakespeare intended the repetition. If the earlier dialogue was meant to stand, then Cassius knows that Brutus knows of Portia's death. He might have been puzzled to hear Brutus deny this knowledge. And, of course, he might then have suspected Brutus of deliberately setting up a Stoic opportunity for himself. Various ways out of these difficulties suggest themselves. Cassius might have assumed that Brutus was answering Messala's question literally—that he had received no letters mentioning Portia's death but had heard of it by other means. Or Cassius might have been so impressed by Brutus's self-control in the earlier dialogue that he failed to notice that Brutus was now claiming to have heard nothing of the matter. Cassius's worship of Brutus is, after all, a significant blind spot in Cassius's usually clearsighted perceptions.

As is often the case, a carefully thought-out performance can shed light on a textual problem. Here the rescuer is also Trevor Nunn's 1972 *Julius Caesar*. Nunn retained both passages. "As Messala speaks of Portia, Brutus signals to

Cassius to keep silence. His dialogue with Messala is a public shield against the privacy of his grief being further invaded, and Cassius is the one sharer of the secret of Brutus's prior knowledge and real feelings. This second, personal conspiracy seals the bond of brotherhood that has just been renewed between them."[6]

Readers who wish to experience *Julius Caesar* directly from the First Folio may do so without difficulty. Several facsimile editions exist. Scholars generally prefer the *Norton Facsimile*, edited by Charlton Hinman (1968, 2nd ed., with additional commentary by Peter Blaney, 1996). Unlike its predecessors, this edition was not compiled by photographing the pages of a copy of the First Folio. Here each of the pages was selected individually, from the numerous copies of the First Folio owned by the Folger Shakespeare Library, for its clarity and its freedom from stains, smudges, typographical errors, show-through from the reverse page, and other obstacles to immediate connection with the text.

LATER FOLIO TEXTS AND THE DOUAI MANUSCRIPT

Although the First Folio text of *Julius Caesar* is free of major problems, it is still very different from the texts generally used today. In this section, we take a quick look at the evolution of the modern scholarly edition, as this concept applies to Shakespeare's work in general and *Julius Caesar* in particular.

Throughout the seventeenth century, publishers responded to the public demand for Shakespeare's works by replicating what they already had in hand. The First Folio was republished in 1632, 1663, and 1685; in each case, the printer set up his type by consulting a previous edition. There are differences among the editions, some for the better and some for the worse, as printers corrected obvious errors and then made new ones of their own, but none of these differences is of significance to our concerns with *Julius Caesar*.

In the late seventeenth century, *Julius Caesar* was published several times by itself in a small one-play quarto format. These quartos were set up from folio editions already in print; they have no bearing on the text of the play itself. However, their existence is evidence of the play's popularity.

Another evidence of *Julius Caesar*'s popularity is its inclusion in Douai Manuscript 7.87, a manuscript collection of six of Shakespeare's plays transcribed by hand from the Second Folio (1632) in 1694 or 1695.[7] This transcript was apparently used in amateur stage productions. (Besides *Julius Caesar*, the manuscript includes *Twelfth Night*, *As You Like It*, *The Comedy of Errors*, *Romeo and Juliet*, and *Macbeth*.)

The Douai text includes some stage directions not in the Second Folio, indicative, scholars assume, of the acting practices of the time and also aligned with common sense, as this example from Act II will demonstrate. The conspirators are preparing to escort Caesar to the Capitol, thus ensuring that he will be on hand to meet his fate. Caesar greets them by name:

... what, Trebonius:
I have an hour's talk in store for you.
Remember that you call on me today.
Be near me, that I may remember you.   (II.ii.120–125)

The Douai text adds the stage direction "aside" at the appropriate place in Trebonius's reply:

Caesar, I will; [*aside*] and so near will I be
That your best friends shall wish I had been further.

EIGHTEENTH-CENTURY EDITIONS: ACT AND SCENE DIVISIONS

Julius Caesar's textual history in the eighteenth century includes further addition of stage directions, the provision of notes and other scholarly apparatus, and the division of the First Folio's five acts into component scenes.

As a background to these developments, we need to note that the eighteenth century saw a change in the way English literature was regarded. More people were being educated, the reading public was larger (although the concept of universal literacy was still far in the future), and scholars who had assumed that only Greek or Latin literature was worthy of study began to take a more appreciative look at the productions of their native land. The result was an outpouring of editions of earlier English literature, often with introductions, critical commentary, notes on words that had become unfamiliar or obsolete, and in general the kind of explanatory apparatus to which we are accustomed today. (These techniques had already been developed for use by Latin and Greek scholars.) Spelling and punctuation were typically standardized as well. Seventeenth-century practice in these areas had been somewhat haphazard.

One of the earliest of these editors, Nicholas Rowe (1674–1718), was well suited for his task, being a playwright himself; his *Jane Shore, The Fair Penitent*, and *Lady Jane Grey* still appear in eighteenth-century drama anthologies. Rowe's six-volume edition of Shakespeare's works was published in 1709. For *Julius Caesar*, Rowe provided a list of characters, the *dramatis personae*, and also added numerous stage directions to those already present in the First Folio and its descendants. Here Rowe relied on his own experience as a playwright. He was particularly conscientious in getting people on and off the stage at appropriate points in the action. For example, Rowe makes sure Caesar's ghost exits (IV.iii.286) just before Brutus says he does: "Now I have taken heart thou vanishest." The fact, incidentally, that the Folio text has brought the ghost onto the stage but neglected to get him off again might be explained by the assumption that the text was derived from a prompt copy. An actor waiting backstage might well need a reminder as to when he needs to go on; but once on and involved in the action, he would hardly forget to make his exit.

The question of adding stage directions to Shakespeare's text is far from closed and in fact remains controversial. Many scholars and editors feel that the text itself tells readers what is going on—who is kneeling to whom, who is stabbing whom—and that readers should use their imagination. Both examples just cited, Trebonius's aside and Caesar's ghost's exit, are implied by the dialogue itself. (Rowe, who had not consulted the Douai manuscript, independently gives Trebonius the same aside. This agreement would suggest that anyone reading the text carefully will visualize the appropriate actions as they occur.) On the other side of the question are those who feel that readers of Shakespeare have enough work to do as it is, and editors who supply ready-made stage directions lighten the load in a constructive manner.

Another category of Rowe's editorial undertakings, one that permanently altered the look of *Julius Caesar*'s text, was the division into separate scenes of the five acts found in the First Folio. Taken as a whole, the First Folio had been inconsistent in this regard. Some of the plays are fully supplied with act and scene divisions; *As You Like It* and several of the other comedies are among these. Other plays—*Romeo and Juliet*, for example—have no act or scene divisions at all in the First Folio. The text just keeps going. *Hamlet* is an intermediate case, with acts and scenes indicated as far as II.ii, when divisions stop.

As far as a theater audience is concerned, these divisions are artificial. Shakespeare's theater had no proscenium curtain to lower and raise to mark the acts, and scholars agree that although there may have been occasional pauses, the plays were essentially acted straight through. The division of a published text into acts (usually five of them) was an editorial custom based on classical precedent; Seneca's tragedies, for example, had traditionally been set up in this way. The further subdivision of the text into scenes derives from a somewhat more flexible tradition. In English drama, the idea of a scene is connected to that of time and place; the action within a scene is continuous, and the location does not change.

This distinction would seem an easy one to apply, but in fact a few quibbles exist. *Julius Caesar* gives us two instances in which characters begin a scene in an exterior space, then move to a nearby interior. Caesar and his companions, at the beginning of Act III, come onstage at a spot just outside the Capitol building, and then enter the building. The text as it is now usually printed, following the scene divisions established by Rowe and by other eighteenth-century editors, continues as the same scene. ("Caesar enters the Capitol, the rest following," the stage direction marking the transition in many modern editions, was supplied by George Steevens, following the example of Edward Capell, whose edition of Shakespeare was published in 1760.) But again, in IV.ii, Cassius and Brutus meet and begin an acrimonious exchange at a spot outside Brutus's tent. At Brutus's suggestion, they move inside, and this time the text as it is usually printed does begin a new scene.

Not surprisingly, editors past and present have occasionally rebelled against the scene divisions Rowe and his successors established and have substituted their own arrangement. The problem that then arises is one of convenience and communication. Dividing one scene into two, or merging two scenes into one, even if supremely logical to the editor making the change, disrupts all the other numbers and makes it difficult to cite quotations in accord with standard usage. What one may learn from pondering this difficulty, to which there is no simple solution, is that editing Shakespeare is a great deal more complicated than it might seem.

Another project undertaken by Rowe and other editors of his era is also subject to controversy. This task involved the labeling of scene locations—for example, "Rome: A street" (I.i), "Rome: Caesar's house" (II.ii), and "The plains of Philippi" (V.i). Editors today may choose to follow their own opinions and vary these designations, or they may dispense with them entirely, on the ground that they do not exist in the First Folio. Again, the question arises as to whether these labels provide a useful service to readers or merely encourage lazy reading habits, since location, like physical action, can generally be deduced from the dialogue.

Among the many other eighteenth-century men of letters who, on their own or in collaboration, brought out editions of Shakespeare's works were poet and critic Alexander Pope and all-around literary lion Samuel Johnson. Editing Shakespeare was a favorite enterprise in this lively literary age.

NINETEENTH-CENTURY EDITIONS: THE VARIORUM CONCEPT

In both England and America, the nineteenth century saw a great rise in middle-class prosperity and leisure. Among the beneficiaries was Shakespeare. His plays held the stage, and his printed works held an honored place in the middle-class family library. Popularity, of course, had its perils. The nineteenth century also saw the editorial labors of Thomas Bowdler, whose *Family Shakespeare* (1807 and 1818) carefully omitted, according to the lengthy original title, "those words and expressions . . . which cannot with propriety be read aloud in a family." *Julius Caesar*, having no overt sex to shock a company of ladies, escaped major excisions.

Family values aside, nineteenth-century editors generally built on the work of their predecessors and were especially diligent in philological commentary on archaic words and in seeking out Shakespeare's literary sources. The idea of the "variorum" edition, in particular, flourished during this century. A variorum edition lists the variant readings of a text, often a complicated matter, though of less moment in *Julius Caesar*, and also assembles annotation and commentary by various earlier writers. A variorum edition allows one to look up, say, a single line in a single scene, and then to see at a glance a great deal of information about that line.

The first Shakespeare Variorum, published in 1803, was edited by Isaac Reed, though his work was based on Steevens's earlier edition. The Second Variorum was essentially a reprint of the first; the Third Variorum, edited by James Boswell the younger, came out in 1821 and brought together a great deal of previous commentary.

The Fourth Shakespeare Variorum, and the last of this category to be mentioned here because it is still under way, was begun in 1871 by Horace H. Furness, then continued by his son, H. H. Furness, Jr. In 1936 the Modern Language Association of America undertook the continuation of the project. *Julius Caesar* occupies volume 17, published in 1913. The contents are dated, especially from a critical perspective, and often seem quaintly worded. Nevertheless, it is often worth consulting. A bibliographical supplement was compiled by John W. Velz in 1977.

CURRENTLY AVAILABLE EDITIONS OF *JULIUS CAESAR*

The *Julius Caesar* texts discussed in this section are those currently in print and available from publishers or in bookshops. These fall into two categories. Editions of Shakespeare's complete works usually include considerable scholarly apparatus, as well as the texts themselves. Editions of the separate plays, including *Julius Caesar*, are typically small, inexpensive, and easily portable, though generally well edited and supplied with useful notes. This is by no means a complete list. In making it, I have kept in mind general readers who like immediate and full explanations of puzzling points. Editions not included here may nevertheless be perfectly adequate for the purposes of many readers.

The one-volume *Riverside Shakespeare* (Boston: Houghton Mifflin, 1974; 2nd ed., 1997), edited by G. Blakemore Evans, gives the complete works in modern American spelling. Brutus is an "honorable man," not an "honourable man." Like most other present-day editions, the text distinguishes betweeen those "ed" endings that are to be pronounced and those that are not—a useful aid for understanding the rhythm, especially when reading aloud. In this case, the syllabic "ed" is spelled out, while the nonsyllabic "ed" is indicated with an apostrophe—for example, "Through this the well-beloved Brutus stabb'd." Textual notes follow each play, arranged by scene and line, explaining any variation between the original text(s) and that of the Riverside edition. These notes, the most complete of any easily available source, also document textual contributions by early editors (Rowe, etc.). Explanatory notes appear at the bottom of each page, keyed to the appropriate line of text. These define difficult words or phrases, give background information, and supply cross-references. The second edition has augmented the scholarly apparatus and critical essays pertaining to Shakespeare's works as a whole. With regard to *Julius Caesar*, however, there is essentially no difference between the two editions; the text, notes, and introductory essay (by Frank Kermode) are unchanged.

David Bevington's *The Complete Works of Shakespeare*, 4th ed. (New York: HarperCollins, 1991), in one volume, is a pleasure to read for physical as well as intellectual reasons, having been set in unusually large and clear type. Spelling is modern and American. Explanatory notes are given on the page with the text. Textual notes are gathered at the back of the volume; those on *Julius Caesar* are very brief, giving only variations between Bevington's text and the First Folio. All introductions to the individual plays are by the editor. A new edition has been announced as forthcoming.

William Shakespeare: The Complete Works (Oxford: Clarendon Press, 1986), edited by Stanley Wells and Gary Taylor, occupies two volumes, one reproducing the original spelling and the other with modernized (British) spelling. Both volumes include a general introduction by Wells and a brief glossary of difficult words. There are no explanatory notes, although each volume has a brief introduction. Textual notes appear in a third volume, *William Shakespeare: A Textual Companion* (Oxford: Clarendon Press, 1987). For *Julius Caesar*, these textual notes are clearly written and include references to previous scholarship.

The *Norton Shakespeare* (New York: Norton, 1997), a one-volume edition of the complete works, is based on the modern-spelling Wells and Taylor text and is supplied with explanatory notes and designed for classroom use. The general editor is Stephen Greenblatt. The textual and explanatory notes are not as full as those of the Riverside or the David Bevington one-volume edition. The introductory essay for *Julius Caesar* is by Katharine Eisaman Maus.

Individual editions of *Julius Caesar* are often part of a series including all or most of Shakespeare's plays. Usually the series itself is overseen by a general editor, while individual titles may be edited by other scholars. The following choices, all available in paperback, do not comprise a complete list but are particularly useful for secondary school and college students.

The Signet Classic Shakespeare's *Julius Caesar* (1963, 1987), edited by William and Barbara Rosen under the general editorship of Sylvan Barnet, uses modern American spelling. Explanatory notes appear at the bottom of each page. There is a brief note on the text. Supplementary material includes extracts from Thomas North's translation of Plutarch's *Lives of the Noble Grecians and Romans*, Shakespeare's main source for this play; a performance history by Sylvan Barnet; and critical commentary by Maynard Mack, Ernest Schanzer, Roy Walker, Richard David, and Ralph Berry.

The New Folger Library's *Julius Caesar* (1992), edited by Barbara Mowat and Paul Werstine, arranges the text on the recto (right) side of each leaf, with notes and other related material facing the text on the verso (left) of the previous leaf. These notes include an opening summary of each scene. Spelling is modernized and American. For a small paperback, this edition makes unusually full use of illustrations, often woodcuts from contemporary books in the Folger Shakespeare Library's collection. Supplementary material includes an essay, "*Julius Caesar*: A Modern Perspective," by Coppélia Kahn, an annotated bibliography, and material on Shakespeare's life, language, and theater.

The Bantam Classics series of Shakespeare's works is edited by David Bevington, who also wrote the introductions. Each play has a foreword by Joseph Papp on the performance aspect. *Julius Caesar* (New York: Bantam Books, 1980, 1988) includes extracts from Plutarch and an annotated bibliography. Explanatory notes appear on each page, and there is a separate note on the text. Spelling is American.

The Arden Shakespeare's *Julius Caesar*, edited by T. S. Dorsch (London and New York: Routledge, 1955; repr. 1988), stems from a British enterprise founded in the 1890s. The original Arden Shakespeare, a thirty-seven-volume work, was completed in 1924 and became a standard scholarly reference through its accurate text and extensive notes. A revision, the New Arden Shakespeare, was undertaken in 1951. Older material was replaced to such an extent that the revision became, in effect, a new edition. Dorsch's *Julius Caesar* includes extensive extracts from Plutarch and detailed explanatory notes, many of which deal with textual questions and refer to earlier editions of the play. The editor's thorough introduction discusses sources, language and imagery, characterization, and other relevant matters. A third series of the Arden Shakespeare editions is currently under way; *Julius Caesar*, edited by David Daniell, is available as of June, 1998.

The New Cambridge Shakespeare's *Julius Caesar*, edited by Marvin Spevack (Cambridge: Cambridge University Press, 1988), emphasizes the performance aspect of the play and includes drawings of scenes from *Julius Caesar* as they might have been staged at Shakespeare's Globe, as conjectured by scholar-artist C. Walter Hodges. Illustrations also include photographs from recent stage and screen productions of the play. Spelling is British. Extracts from Plutarch are included. Textual and explanatory notes appear on each page.

Arthur Humphreys has edited *Julius Caesar* for the World's Classics Series (Oxford: Oxford University Press, 1994), supplying a lengthy and well-organized introduction. Explanatory and textual notes appear on each page; spelling is British. Passages from Plutarch are included.

NOTES

1. T. S. Dorsch, in the *Arden Shakespeare: Julius Caesar* (London: Routledge, 1955, repr. 1988), gives a scholarly and readable account of the text. See pp. xxiii–xxvi.

2. Arthur Humphreys, ed., *Julius Caesar* (Oxford: Oxford University Press, 1984, repr. 1994), p. 74.

3. In Jonson's *Timber, or Discoveries Made upon Men and Matter*. See Humphreys, *Julius Caesar*, pp. 4–5, 82–83.

4. Ralph Berry, "On Directing Shakespeare: An Interview with Trevor Nunn, Director of the Royal Shakespeare Company," in William Rosen and Barbara Rosen, eds., *Julius Caesar* (New York: Signet, 1987), p. 229.

5. See Warren D. Smith, "The Duplicate Revelation of Portia's Death," *SQ* 4 (1935), 153–161, and Brents Stirling, "*Julius Caesar* in Revision," *SQ* 13 (1962), 187–205.

6. Richard David, "A Review of *Julius Caesar*" (Royal Shakespeare, 1972), in Rosen and Rosen, *Julius Caesar*, p. 225.

7. See G. Blakemore Evans, "The Douai Manuscript—Six Shakespeare Transcripts," *PQ* 41 (1962), 158–172. The manuscript is in the public library at Douai, France.

2

CONTEXTS AND SOURCES

In this chapter we explore the context of *Julius Caesar* as a historical event in itself and as a play performed for an Elizabethan audience. We also look at Shakespeare's sources, in particular Plutarch's biographies of notable Greeks and Romans as translated by Thomas North.

THE WORLD OF SHAKESPEARE'S AUDIENCE: PLAYHOUSES AND POLITICS

On a September afternoon in 1599, one Thomas Platter, a Swiss medical student visiting London, went with his friends across the Thames and "there in the house with the thatched roof witnessed an excellent performance of the tragedy of the first Emperor Julius Caesar."[1] Here we might make a brief detour to point out that Platter's identification of Julius Caesar as an emperor should not be held against him as evidence of Platter's ignorance or that of sixteenth-century playgoers in general. People make this mistake every day. It was Julius Caesar's grand nephew and immediate heir, Octavius Caesar, later known as Augustus Caesar, who became the first Roman emperor. "Caesar" started out simply as a family name, but it then became a title used by succeeding emperors and thus brings about an understandable confusion.[2]

Platter goes on to describe the playgoing activity of London:

> Thus daily at two in the afternoon, London has two, sometimes three plays running in different places, competing with each other, and those which play best obtain most spectators. The playhouses are so constructed that they play on a raised platform, so that everyone has a good view. There are different galleries and places, however, where the seating is better and more comfortable and therefore more expensive.[3]

Going to the theater in 1599. Sketch by Jo McMurtry, 1997, based in part on the reconstructed Shakespeare's Globe in London.

As Platter's description implies, the public theaters and the custom of attending them were a unique feature of London life. If Swiss cities had had similar facilities, Platter would not have bothered to paint those of London in such detail.

Since London playgoers were accustomed to evaluating the offerings of the Globe along with those of its South Bank rivals, including in 1599 the Swan and the Rose, they would seem to have been a sophisticated body, at least with regard to theatrical matters. Recent scholarship has upheld this idea. Ann Jennalie Cook describes Shakespeare's audience as above the norm in education, affluence, and general alertness.[4] Andrew Gurr presents evidence from contemporary documents that the Globe was perceived as a prestigious (and expensive) venue.[5] It is true that the "groundlings," standing in the Globe's open courtyard, got their entertainment cheaply, but these were a fairly small proportion of the total audience. Playgoers occupying the galleries paid for their comfort, as Platter remarked.

What might have been the concerns of this urban and sophisticated audience in 1599?[6] What did they talk about on their way to the playhouse, and what resonance might the underlying ideas of *Julius Caesar*—political power and assassination, for example—have had in the lives of those who gathered to hear the play?

Politically, the atmosphere was quietly dramatic, filled with unspoken (or, perhaps, spoken-only-in-private) suspense. Queen Elizabeth I, aging but energetic, was on the throne she had occupied since 1558. Her reign had been peaceful and prosperous by the standards of the day, but it was clearly approaching its close, and the great disadvantage of a virgin queen is that she can leave no eldest son, no indisputable heir.

Questions of the transfer of power and the preservation of social order may have teased at the minds of the audience as they fixed their attention on ancient Rome. Must they themselves look forward to chaos, bloodshed, and the dogs of war? Disputes over the English crown had been the subject of Shakespeare's history plays, written earlier in the 1590s. Would the present audience, many of whom had seen the English histories enacted by the same company now bringing *Julius Caesar* to life, find themselves hurled from their peaceful and prosperous seats, so to speak, and forced to act in a real-life revival of the Wars of the Roses?

Another type of contemporary resonance with *Julius Caesar* might well have proceeded simply from the idea of political assassination, never absent in human history. Only fifteen years earlier, in 1584, William I of Orange, Protestant leader of the Netherlands' revolt against Spanish rule and an English ally, had been assassinated by a fanatical Catholic. In France, where dynastic conflict was raging, the year 1588 had seen the assassinations of Henry, duke of Guise, and his brother, Louis, cardinal of Guise; both killings had been ordered by the French king, Henry III, who in turn had been assassinated the following year.

Queen Elizabeth herself was not safe from the threat of assassination. Her peaceful death in 1603 is known to us, naturally, but not to the original audience of *Julius Caesar*, to whom she was still alive and therefore vulnerable. In the early 1570s, Pope Pius V had pronounced that all Catholic subjects were released from allegiance to "Elizabeth, the Pretended Queen of England"—in other words, he had nominated her as an approved assassination target.[7] The queen continued to go about in public as usual, but plots against her life were discovered from time to time.

Audiences at the Globe after 1603, when Queen Elizabeth had been succeeded by King James I, would have continued their awareness of the contemporary reality of assassination. In 1605, the king came within a hair of being blown up along with his entire Parliament; the discovery of the Gunpowder Plot, just in time, is still celebrated as Guy Fawkes Day (November 5). Across the English Channel, France had not calmed down either. Henry IV, successor to Henry III, though not closely related, was assassinated in 1610.

"HOW DID THEY EVER THINK THEY WOULD GET AWAY WITH IT?"

This question is often asked by present-day readers of *Julius Caesar* and may have been asked by the Elizabethans as well. How in the world could the conspirators expect to stab somebody to death, walk to the marketplace waving their bloody swords and shouting, "Peace, freedom and liberty!" and escape being clapped into the nearest jail?

We need to consider two aspects of this matter. The civilization of Rome in 44 B.C. was different from that of today's world. Also, Shakespeare had pushed the pace of the action by condensing some events and omitting others, and consequently the abruptness we find so disconcerting was less so in historical reality. The more educated portion of Shakespeare's audience would presumably have been aware of this discrepancy. Presumably, also, they would have realized the extent to which Shakespeare's compression of time had heightened the dramatic impact of the play and would not have been distressed by it. Shakespeare was, after all, writing a work of art, not a historical treatise.

Apart from these complications, Americans pondering *Julius Caesar* are subject to a special perplexity because of our associations with the architectural style of ancient Rome. We connect marble columns, domes, pediments, and similar classical motifs with justice, objectivity, and the rule of law. This juxtaposition results from deliberate policy. Eighteenth- and nineteenth-century American architects chose Roman models for government buildings, especially those connected with lawmaking and the courts, in order to invoke the idea of the Roman Republic, where, in theory at least, government was representative, power was balanced, and no one man could gain total control. (Ironically, the grandiose marble buildings so beloved of architects are less typical of the Roman Republic than of its immediate successor in history, the Roman Empire.) Americans thus have some difficulty in suspending disbelief when asked, first, to envision a bloody and deliberate murder committed in a setting reminiscent of our nation's Capitol building or the Supreme Court building across the street, and, second, to envision the perpetrators then assuming they would be hailed as the saviors of their country.

Architecture aside, Americans tend to make other assumptions that lead astray our responses to *Julius Caesar*. The Roman Senate, for example, was not directly elected by the populace. In 44 B.C., its membership included aristocrats from old families, according to what had become Roman tradition. It also contained a great many newcomers appointed by Julius Caesar, a development that infuriated the traditional senators but that they were powerless to stop, since several of Caesar's official titles allowed him to add members to the Senate. Caesar had formed the habit of holding a number of public offices simultaneously, and this too angered the traditionalists.

Another significant difference between the Roman Senate and the similarly named bodies with which we are now more familiar had to do with power. The Roman Senate could rule by decree, and it could impose such penalties as death, exile, and forfeiture of property.

The conspiracy itself was larger than Shakespeare implies. Today's scholars, after consulting historical documents, generally agree on a figure of sixty.[8] Only a few of these actually did the deed, thus getting their names into the history books and eventually appearing as characters in Shakespeare's play.

Keeping these facts in mind, we need to look at the actual events, particularly those immediately following the assassination, which Shakespeare drastically telescopes. In the play, the assassination scene (III.i) is immediately followed by the Forum scene, in which Brutus and Antony take turns speaking to the people. In reality these events covered a space of several days.

Immediately after Caesar was stabbed to death in the Capitol, the city was gripped by panic, and many Romans, including Antony, fled to their houses or the houses of friends. Shakespeare touches on this reaction but skips the less dramatic period that followed, beginning with an indecisive lull. Everyone waited to see what would happen. Some of Caesar's servants took his body to his house. The conspirators occupied the Capitol. They apparently had made no firm plans for what they would do after the murder; their aim was to restore the Roman Republic in some earlier form, but specific steps in that direction had not been determined. They did go briefly out into the marketplace, presumably hoping for enthusiastic acclaim from the populace, but they found instead an atmosphere of shock and caution. The assassins were not arrested when they made this appearance because no authority was empowered to do so. As senators, *they* were the authorities.

At some point after the assassination, Lepidus, a general whose legion happened to be stationed just outside Rome, visited Antony and offered to send his soldiers against the conspirators.[9] Antony must have been greatly heartened by this asset. Shakespeare does not mention Lepidus or his convenient army at this point in the story, but he does show Lepidus shortly afterward as a triumvir, along with Antony and Octavius Caesar, after the conspirators had fled Rome (IV.i).

Antony decided against using large-scale force, however. He did not know how many influential Romans might have been in sympathy with the conspirators, but no doubt he suspected that this group might be large and dangerous. Also, he wanted to get the Roman people on his side, a task that might be difficult if he immediately undertook what might turn into a military occupation. Passions would more easily be calmed if he moved within an orderly framework. Antony at the time was serving as consul, a post that empowered him to call the Senate into session, and he announced a meeting for the next morning.

As Antony had probably guessed, a large number of the senators were sympathetic to the conspirators. Caesar, they claimed, had been a tyrant; he had usurped power and violated Roman ideals and therefore deserved death. "Aristocratic Romans," as Michael Grant has pointed out, "had long been brought up to regard it as their duty to kill tyrants."[10] Further detail is supplied by Frank Burr Marsh:

> The Romans were not original thinkers, and the educated class had taken over without serious question the ethics of the Greeks. From the old city-states of Greece, where tyrannies had been a standing menace to every form of government, there had been derived the maxim that the slaying of a tyrant was not only a righteous act but a positive duty of the patriotic citizen. By a tyrant the Greeks meant a ruler, whatever his character, who gained the supreme power by illegal means and by the subversion of the constitution of his country. . . . The only question which could occur to a cultured Roman trained in Greek ethics, as practically all were trained, was whether Caesar came within the definition of a tyrant.[11]

A tyrant, it was felt, transformed himself into a public enemy by seizing power in an illegal manner. Although it was true that Caesar's powers had been granted him by the Senate and the people, his enemies could argue that Caesar in various ways had extorted these favors, that they were not freely given.

As the Senate pondered this matter, Antony pointed out that to proclaim Caesar a tyrant would mean that all his acts were illegal, and some of these acts had been beneficial to the very senators who now applauded his death. "Were all his honorable colleagues prepared voluntarily to relinquish the appointments and titles granted them by a usurper in violation of the law?"[12]

The Senate, caught in a bind, resolved the dilemma by the illogical but practical solution of pardoning the assassins without proclaiming Caesar an illegal usurper or nullifying Caesar's acts. Shakespeare refers to this decision briefly in Brutus's speech in the Forum: "The question of his death is enroll'd in the Capitol; his glory not extenuated, wherein he was worthy; nor his offences enforc'd [emphasized], for which he suffer'd death" (III.ii.37–40).

Antony then pressed another point. Among the many offices Caesar had held was that of *pontifex maximus*, or high priest. As a mark of respect for the official Roman religion, then, Caesar deserved a state funeral.[13] The Senate agreed. Antony begged permission to speak at the funeral. And at this point we find ourselves back in Shakespeare's story.

JULIUS CAESAR IN THE POPULAR IMAGINATION: HERO OR VILLAIN?

Did Shakespeare's audience sympathize with Julius Caesar, treacherously slain by his supposed friends, or with Brutus and his fellow conspirators, liberating their country from the iron grasp of tyranny? This question is, of course, too simple. The play derives its dramatic tension from ambiguity. The audience's mind is meant to seesaw, pull about, and seek some sort of balance, aware the whole time of the complexity of the issues.[14]

This ambiguity, this mixture of reactions, has a long pedigree. It goes back to the historical moment itself, to the Ides of March in the year 44 B.C., when opinions of Caesar covered a wide range. Caesar had risen to unprecedented heights. He had conquered Gaul and begun the conquest of England, had fought a civil war against his erstwhile colleague Gnaeus Pompey, and had rearranged the power structure of republican Rome by forcing the Senate to declare him dictator for life. He would naturally have accumulated both loyal friends and bitter enemies. These friends or enemies made their opinions known, often in writing. Some of these writings then came down through the generations, crossing geographical and linguistic boundaries, to settle into the curriculum of Stratford Grammar School, where Shakespeare and his classmates read them along with other specimens of the Latin literature so strongly emphasized in Elizabethan education.[15]

Among Caesar's major enemies during his lifetime was Cicero (106–43 B.C.), orator and philosopher, whose writings were studied during the Renaissance as choice examples of Latin style. Cicero appears briefly in Shakespeare's play (I.ii, I.iii) and is nominated, though rejected, as a member of the conspiracy (II.i.41). This dialogue is in accordance with history; Cicero was not in on the plot. He nevertheless greeted Caesar's death with unmixed delight. Writing to one of the conspirators after the assassination, he said, "I congratulate you. I rejoice for myself. I love you. I watch your interests; I wish for your love and to be informed what you are doing and what is being done."[16]

Of the writings of another of Caesar's enemies, Marcus Cato (95–46 B.C.), only a letter to Cicero has survived, and Cato's anti-Caesar sympathies influenced succeeding generations chiefly through his reputation for virtue and honesty. In Shakespeare's play, he is mentioned as the father of Brutus's wife, Portia (II.i.295), and of the "Young Cato" who dies at the battle of Philippi (V.iv.5). His name also comes up in the context of committing suicide when facing military defeat (V.i.101), a program Cato had followed after supporting Pompey against Caesar.

On the other side of the question was Julius Caesar himself, whose works were also part of the educated person's academic experience in sixteenth-century England. Caesar's *Commentaries*, including a history of the Gallic wars and a partial history of the war against Pompey, not surprisingly present the author as a judicious, efficient, and forceful person of courage and vision. This impression was not all a matter of managed propaganda. External facts bear it out; Julius Caesar was an amazing human being, a military genius, one of the extraordinary figures of world history. His *Commentaries*, moreover, achieve their self-serving effects in a subtle manner. Caesar's writing style is simple, factual, and dignified. A reader immersed in his book might naturally feel close to the author, see the world from his perspective, and come to sympathize with him.

Another pro-Caesar writer, Ovid (43 B.C.–A.D. 17), familiar to Elizabethan schoolboys through his collection of Greek and Roman legends, the *Metamorphoses*, lived in the time of Augustus Caesar ("Octavius" in Shakespeare's play). As Julius Caesar's heir, Augustus naturally favored positive views of his predecessor, and Ovid obliged. The *Metamorphoses* ends with Ovid's fanciful account of the assassination. The goddess Venus, from whom Caesar's family claimed legendary descent, was dreadfully upset when she learned that Caesar was destined to be murdered, but Jove insisted that the decrees of fate could not be altered. Venus then:

> Amid the Senate house of Rome invisible did stand,
> And from her Caesar's body took his new expulsed sprite,
> The which she not permitting to resolve to air quite,
> Did place it in the sky among the stars that glister bright,
> And as she bare it, she did feel it gather heavenly might,
> And for to waxen fiery. She no sooner let it fly,
> But that a goodly shining star it up aloft did sty [ascend],
> And drew a great way after it bright beams like burning hair.   (XV.949–956)[17]

Caesar's literal transformation into a star does not appear in Shakespeare's *Julius Caesar*, but this passage may have influenced some of the play's cosmic imagery. Caesar's description of himself as "constant as the northern star" (III.i.60) may be a reminiscence of this passage.[18] Again, Ovid's description of the star's drawing after it "bright beams like burning hair" sounds very like a comet, and several ancient sources tell of a comet that appeared after the assassination.[19] Shakespeare's Calphurnia foreshadows this event when she tells Caesar, "When beggars die there are no comets seen" (II.ii.30).

Varied views of Julius Caesar continued to perpetuate themselves through the Middle Ages. Dante (1265–1321) saw Brutus and Cassius as deeply dyed traitors, disloyal to their friend and ruler, and in his *Inferno* gives them a central place in hell; Satan holds them in his mouth, along with Judas Iscariot, betrayer of Christ (Canto xxxiv, 61–67). Although there is no evidence that Shakespeare read Dante, both poets, according to Francis Fergusson, shared a kinship based on their medieval heritage.[20]

Medieval literature was not universally pro-Caesar, however. In works of the "De Casibus" (literally, "in the case of") tradition, typically a string of stories about or references to famous men who fell from the heights of glory, Caesar appears in a more doubtful light. The unifying theme was the fickleness of Fortune, usually a strongly personified figure; but while Fortune could be said to pick her victims capriciously, the medieval love of moralizing furthered the implication that the victim somehow brought his fate upon himself. Geoffrey Chaucer (1342–1400) mentions Caesar in the *Canterbury Tales* ("Monk's Tale," 2671–2726), though Chaucer's narrating monk blames Fortune primarily and praises Caesar's manly heart. Edmund Spenser (1552–1599), however, places Caesar and his associates among a pile of ancient Romans occupying the dungeon of the allegorical House of Pride: "High Caesar, great Pompey, and fiers Antonius" (*The Faerie Queene*, I.v.49). Again, *The Mirror for Magistrates*, a collection of "De Casibus" tales by various writers, added a piece on Julius Caesar in the edition of 1587. Here Caesar is seen quite unsympathetically. The closing stanza suggests the tone:

> But since my whole pretense was glory vain,
> To have renown and rule above the rest,
> Without remorse of many thousands slain,
> Which, for their own defense, their wars addressed,
> I deem therefore my stony heart and breast
> Received so many wounds for just revenge; they stood
> By justice right of Jove, the sacred sentence good:
> That who so slays, he pays the price, is blood for blood.[21]

Prideful tyrant or innocent victim, then, or something in between, Caesar may wear many labels. Shakespeare follows this tradition of ambiguity as he creates his own Caesar.

PLUTARCH AND HIS *PARALLEL LIVES*

Plutarch's biographical works are the main source for *Julius Caesar*, although scholars have suggested that Shakespeare consulted various other classical historians.[22] It is also possible that Shakespeare knew any of several contemporary plays in which Julius Caesar appears as a character.[23] Plutarch, however, is without question the main source of Shakespeare's play.

A Greek living in the first century A.D., Plutarch arranges his *Parallel Lives* according to a plan that leapfrogs chronology and highlights personality. His biographies of well-known Greeks and Romans are set up in pairs, one Greek with one Roman, and Plutarch includes with each pair a short essay pointing out their similarities and differences. (The pattern is not entirely symmetrical. Forty-six of the fifty biographies are linked; the remaining four are singletons.)

Plutarch pairs Julius Caesar with Alexander the Great (356–323 B.C.), viewing both as conquerors who died young. Brutus has as his Greek partner Dion (c. 408–323 B.C.); both, Plutarch points out, were solidly grounded in philosophy, especially that of Plato, and both tried to free their country from men they perceived as tyrants, Dion having expelled his nephew, Dionysius the Younger, from Syracuse. Mark Antony is paired with Demetrius of Macedonia (c. 336–285 B.C.), both mighty generals notorious for revelry.

Plutarch was well positioned for this enterprise. Although he lived most of his life in his native town in northern Greece, then under Roman rule, he is thought to have spent some time in Rome as a teacher of rhetoric. He was obviously well educated, and scholars assume that he had access to oral traditions as well as written sources. His method of delineation depends heavily on anecdotes, some of them trivial in proportion to the large-scale activities of his subjects, but appropriate nevertheless to Plutarch's emphasis on character and morality. "The noblest deeds do not always show men's virtues and vices, but often times a light occasion, a word, or some sports, makes men's natural dispositions and manners appear more plain, than the famous battles won."[24] This technique would appeal to Shakespeare as he set about turning Plutarch's material into playable scenes and speakable dialogue.

The English translation Shakespeare used was that of Thomas North.[25] North worked not from the original Greek but from a French version by Jacques Amyot, published in 1559. Amyot's translation had been enthusiastically received, influencing, for example, the work of Montaigne.[26] North's *Lives of the Noble Greeks and Romans* first appeared in 1579, a hefty folio of over a thousand pages. It was reprinted in 1595 and frequently thereafter. Scholars have not determined whether Shakespeare used the 1579 or the 1595 edition for *Julius Caesar*.

Plutarch's Major Characters

Scholars are divided in their opinions of what Plutarch actually thought of many of the figures he writes about, particularly Caesar. T.J.B. Spencer, for example, editor of *Shakespeare's Plutarch*, feels that Plutarch neither understood nor liked Caesar. Plutarch "respected the republican virtues of Rome. Caesar was the cause of the downfall of the Republic, and Plutarch does not refrain from expressing his disapproval" (Spencer, p. 14). But Marvin Spevack, editing the New Cambridge *Julius Caesar*, claims that Plutarch's Caesar "is portrayed favorably over a long and illustrious career."[27]

These discrepancies are not surprising. Everything about this historical personage is taut with ambiguity. Moreover, Plutarch wrote about Caesar in three different biographies, Antony's and Brutus's as well as Caesar's own, with varying emphases and varying detail.

In his *Life of Caesar*, Plutarch describes the qualities that made Caesar popular in Rome. He was eloquent in pleading the causes of those he wished to help; he was courteous to everyone he met and generous in hospitality, and he was also respected as a valiant soldier. Before anyone was really aware, Plutarch implies, Caesar had risen to such heights as to inspire discomfort, envy, and hatred, harboring among his ambitions a "covetous desire to be called king" (Spencer, pp. 80–81).

While the consequences of Caesar's desire for kingship comprise the plot of *Julius Caesar*, Shakespeare also dramatizes the courteous and hospitable Caesar. On the morning of his assassination, the conspirators call at his house to escort him to the Capitol. The episode is both ironic and poignant as Caesar greets his callers and offers them a drink:

> Good friends, go in, and taste some wine with me,
> And we, like friends, will straightway go together.   (II.ii.126–127)

Plutarch draws a strong contrast between Brutus and Cassius. Brutus studied philosophy, tried to apply its rules of virtue to his own life, and thereby impressed the populace. Cassius lacked this touch. Thus, Plutarch explains, Brutus was given credit for any noble aspect that might be found in the conspiracy, while Cassius was considered the originator of "all the cruel and violent acts" (Spencer, p. 102). Shakespeare often follows this outline in his characterization of the two. Cassius and the other conspirators, for example, are eager to recruit Brutus because they know he will lend credibility to their enterprise.

Antony appears in Plutarch as a rather paradoxical person. He had a handsome presence; Plutarch, in fact, compares his appearance to representations of Hercules. Antony's soldiers loved him for his courage, good fellowship, and generosity. There were negatives, however. Antony was disliked for "his banquets and drunken feasts. . . . In his house they did nothing but feast, dance, and mask; and himself passed away the time in hearing of foolish plays" (Spencer, p. 102).

Perhaps not surprisingly, Shakespeare does not color Antony's fondness for theater as a bad thing. Instead, this pastime serves to contrast Antony with the less amiable Cassius. In Caesar's words, "He [Cassius] loves no plays / As thou dost, Antony; he hears no music" (I.ii.299–301). For the banquets, too, Caesar shows a somewhat amused tolerance, remarking as Antony enters to escort him to the Capitol, "See! Antony, that revels long a-nights, / Is notwithstanding up" (III.ii.116–117).

Plutarch does not supply the words to Antony's oration at Caesar's funeral, and Shakespeare has an opportunity to use his imagination to extraordinary effect. Plutarch does, however, mention some details of Antony's strategy, including his showing the crowd Caesar's gown, "all bloody in his hand" (Spencer, p. 152).

Calphurnia and Portia in Plutarch

Many of the minor characters who come into Shakespeare's *Julius Caesar* from Plutarch are not particularly dimensional. They exist simply to perform some function for the plot, often a small one. Calphurnia and Portia, the only women in the play, are exceptions to this pattern in that their personalities are more memorable. Calphurnia appears in two scenes; Portia has two scenes and is spoken about in a third. In each case, Shakespeare used many details straight from Plutarch, changed others, and added still others of his own.

Calphurnia's earliest appearance in *Julius Caesar* is very much that—simply an appearance. Her only line is, "Here, my lord" (I.ii.3), spoken in answer to Caesar's calling her name. Caesar goes on to remind Antony to touch Calphurnia as Antony runs the Lupercalian race, a traditional cure, Caesar explains, for barrenness. This exchange is original with Shakespeare, not taken from Plutarch. Among its functions may well be a reminder to the audience of Caesar's kingly ambitions—a point, of course, that Plutarch had raised elsewhere. To the English, accustomed to the transfer of power by way of inheritance, the concept of obtaining a crown is naturally linked to that of founding a dynasty.

For Calphurnia's remaining appearance, Shakespeare does borrow from Plutarch, although he makes some changes. Calphurnia has spent a restless night, with ominous dreams. Plutarch describes two of these dreams. In one, Caesar had been killed and she held his dead body in her arms; in the other, an ornament set on the roof of Caesar's house had broken off, and Calphurnia "lamented and wept for it" (Spencer, p. 89).

Shakespeare's version is different still. As Caesar explains:

> Calphurnia here, my wife, stays me at home:
> She dreamt tonight she saw my statue,
> Which, like a fountain with an hundred spouts,
> Did run pure blood; and many lusty Romans
> Came smiling and did bathe their hands in it.   (II.ii.75–79)

Ironically, this frightening vision is then interpreted by one of the conspirators as "a vision fair and fortunate."

Portia's role is also connected with blood and wounds—her own in this case. The facts are taken from Plutarch. Portia, intent on finding out what was disturbing her husband, sets out to prove to him that she can keep a secret, even should she be tortured. In Plutarch's words, she "took a little razor . . . and, causing her maids and women to go out of her chamber, gave herself a great gash withal in her thigh, that she was straight all of a gore blood" (Spencer, p. 118). Shakespeare stresses Portia's motive more than the blood:

> I have made strong proof of my constancy,
> Giving myself a voluntary wound
> Here, in the thigh; can I bear that with patience
> And not my husband's secrets?   (II.i.229–302)

In both Plutarch and Shakespeare, Brutus is dazzled by this display of stoical endurance and tells her the secret, or some part of it. Plutarch does not give Brutus's words, and in Shakespeare the secret-telling conversation presumably takes place offstage. Portia, in any case, knows enough to be worried when Brutus sets off for the Capitol on the Ides of March. Plutarch describes her going out into the street, sending messengers to find out what Brutus was doing, and finally fainting (Spencer, p. 121). Shakespeare makes use of these suggestions:

> I must go in. Ay me! How weak a thing
> The heart of woman is! O Brutus,
> The heavens speed thee in thine enterprise!

> Sure the boy heard me.—Brutus hath a suit
> That Caesar will not grant.—O, I grow faint—
> Run, Lucius, and commend me to my lord.   (iv.39–44)

Portia does not reappear in *Julius Caesar*, but we hear of her suicide. In Plutarch, she "took hot burning coals and cast them into her mouth, and kept her mouth so close that she choked herself" (Spencer, p. 173). In Shakespeare, she "swallow'd fire" (IV.iii.156).

SHAKESPEARE'S COMPRESSION OF PLUTARCH'S TIME SEQUENCE

Shakespeare's dramatic compression of the events during the day or so immediately following Caesar's assassination has been discussed earlier in this chapter. Shakespeare follows this practice throughout the play, often drastically shortening the time sequence of his source.

The opening scenes, for example, efficiently conflate several actual events. Caesar's triumph upon returning from his campaign in Spain occurred in 45 B.C. Shakespeare merges this occasion with the feast of the Lupercalia, a traditional Roman holiday, the following February (44 B.C.), when, as in Shakespeare's play, Antony offered Caesar a crown but Caesar declined it.

The formation of the conspiracy and the assassination itself seem in Shakespeare's play to take place within a few days. Actually a month has passed. Plutarch, in his life of Brutus, fills this interval by going into detail about the other members of the conspiracy, one by one, as these were recruited by Cassius and then by Brutus. Shakespeare simply has the conspirators appear at Brutus's house, where Cassius introduces them (II.i.90–96).

Immediately after the assassination, the mob seizes and kills an innocent victim, Cinna the Poet. This incident occurs in Plutarch much as it does in the play, including a supernatural touch. Plutarch's Cinna dreams that Caesar had invited him to supper; in Shakespeare, "I dreamt tonight that I did feast with Caesar" (III.iii.1). Plutarch's mob, like Shakespeare's, mistakes the poet for the conspirator, and, "they falling upon him in their rage slew him outright in the market place" (Spencer, p. 130). Shakespeare, however, invents the grim humor of "Tear him for his bad verses!" (30).

Shakespeare makes a great chronological leap forward after Caesar's assassination. In historical time, a year passes between the end of Act III and the beginning of Act IV, when the triumvirate of Octavius, Antony, and Lepidus has settled into power. Much of this year was taken up with a power struggle between Antony and Octavius. Plutarch describes Octavius's leading an army that drove Antony out of Italy, Antony's flight into the Alps, and Antony's eventual return, having won the soldiers of Lepidus's army over to his side (Spencer, p. 193).

Shakespeare resists the urge to include these interesting but complicated developments and directs his own plot toward the confrontation at Philippi. The main clue that some amount of time has passed is that, in the first scene of Act IV, the triumvirs are drawing up an enemy list, and the audience might then assume that some additional events must have occurred in order for them to acquire these enemies.

Plutarch goes into a great deal of detail about Brutus's and Cassius's activities after they flee to Asia, only occasional bits of which Shakespeare used. The two raised armies, built navies, captured cities, and extorted money from any source that came to hand. Shakespeare does use Plutarch's description of the quarrel between Brutus and Cassius (IV.iii), finding a hint for the staging as well as the emotional pitch of the scene. According to Plutarch, the two "went into a little chamber together, and bade every man avoid, and did shut the doors to them. Then they began to pour out their complaints" and "grew hot and loud, earnestly accusing one another, and at length fell both a-weeping" (Spencer, p. 145). Shakespeare gives most of this emotion to Cassius, Brutus remaining calm to the end. And it is only in Shakespeare that Brutus tells Cassius at this point of Portia's death. In Plutarch, this information is not part of a dialogue but is simply given to the reader at another point, in the last few paragraphs of the *Life of Brutus*, as part of a general tying up of loose ends.

Brutus's vision of Caesar's ghost sounds like something Shakespeare might have invented for his Elizabethan audience. However, the incident occurs in Plutarch, although the apparition is not specifically identified as Caesar's ghost. Brutus is sitting in his tent with "a little light," deep in thought; on hearing a sound, he looks at the door and sees "a wonderful strange and monstrous shape." The spirit identifies itself when questioned: "I am thy evil spirit, Brutus; and thou shalt see me by the city of Philippi" (Spencer, p. 149).

Shakespeare uses similar dialogue (IV.iii.275–286), and in fact his text identifies the spirit only in a stage direction: "Enter the ghost of Caesar." Since this direction appears in the First Folio and presumably reflects what was done on Shakespeare's stage, one assumes that the actor playing the part of the ghost had also played Caesar when alive and that the audience was meant to make the connection. Also, Brutus later describes his visitor as "the ghost of Caesar" (V.v.17).

The details of *Julius Caesar*'s final scenes come essentially from Plutarch, with a major change in that Shakespeare conflates the two battles at Philippi, fought almost three weeks apart, into one. The basic outline of Cassius's proposal to delay giving battle and Brutus's overriding him (IV.iii.196–225) appears in Plutarch (Spencer, pp. 152–153).

Shakespeare seems to have been especially alert for personal and emotional details as he read Plutarch's descriptions of what became the final scenes of the play. Cassius's disclaimer to Messala, explaining that he had unwillingly agreed to "set / Upon one battle all our liberties" (V.i.74–75), is part of Plutarch's account in the *Life of Brutus* (Spencer, pp. 153–154), as is Cassius's remark that the day happens to be his birthday. The farewell dialogue between Brutus and Cassius follows, although in Plutarch, Brutus has already made up his mind to kill himself if defeated, while Shakespeare shows him stating first that he would never do such a thing and then, after Cassius reminds him of the disgrace of capture, shifting into the third person and stating that he certainly will:

> Think not, thou noble Roman,
> That ever Brutus will go bound to Rome;
> He bears too great a mind.   (V.i.110–112)

Cassius's error as he watches the battle, supposing that Titinius has been captured when in fact he has met with a group of friends, and Cassius's suicide based on this false supposition, is carefully described in Plutarch. Plutarch mentions Cassius's bad eyesight and gives a vivid description of Titinius's meeting with his comrades: "They shouted out for joy . . . with songs of victory and great rushing of their harness" (Spencer, p. 159). For the suicide itself, in which Cassius is aided by his bondsman Pindarus, Shakespeare alters a rather bizarre detail. In Plutarch's account, Cassius threw his cloak over his head and held out his bare neck to Pindarus. "So the head was found severed from the body" (Spencer, p. 160). Shakespeare has Cassius specify a different modus operandi:

> With this good sword,
> That ran through Caesar's bowels, search this bosom.   (V.iii.41–42)

Presumably a sword thrust was a simpler matter to represent on stage than a decapitation. Another reason for this change may have to do with what we might call supernatural resonance. In Shakespeare, Titinius uses Cassius's sword for his own suicide a few minutes later, when he returns and finds Cassius's body. Brutus then enters, sees the bodies, and exclaims:

> O Julius Caesar, thou art mighty yet!
> Thy spirit walks abroad, and turns our swords
> In our own proper entrails.   (94–96)

In the second battle, which Shakespeare transfers to the afternoon of the same day, Plutarch dwells in detail on Brutus's last moments and portrays the mood as well as the events. The setting is evocative. Brutus passes "a little river walled in on either side and shadowed with great trees" and finally "stayed at the foot of a rock with certain of his captains and friends" (Spencer, p. 169). Shakespeare alludes briefly to this Plutarchian landscape as Brutus says, "Come, poor remains of friends, rest on this rock" (V.v.i).

The details of Brutus's suicide and the honor paid his body by Antony are drawn from Plutarch. Plutarch does not quote Antony's words on this occasion, but Shakespeare supplies a ringing eulogy. In Shakespeare, though not in Plutarch, Octavius then intervenes, rather competitively, taking Brutus's body into his own custody: "Within my tent his bones shall lie tonight" (V.v.78). Shakespeare may have made this addition to emphasize Octavius's superiority over his partner, in his own and history's eyes if not in Antony's. These are the play's closing lines, traditionally spoken (in a tragedy) by the character of highest rank. It is also quite possible that Shakespeare was thinking ahead to the next play he would base on Plutarch, *Antony and Cleopatra*, seven years or so after the first performances of *Julius Caesar*. Here the conflict between Antony and Octavius will come to a head, and Octavius will win.

Shakespeare made many changes in Plutarch's story, only a small proportion of which have been discussed in this chapter. Yet it is the similarities that are striking. Perhaps this is not surprising. Both Plutarch and Shakespeare were interested in large-scale events that changed the course of history. But both were interested primarily in the personalities of the people who caused or found themselves caught up in these events. In Plutarch's biographies and Shakespeare's plays, character and plot are intrinsically interwoven. As Harley Granville-Barker puts it, "Plutarch's genius, in fact, is closely allied to Shakespeare's own, with its power to make, by a touch or so of nature, great men and simple, present and past, the real and the mimic world, one kin."[28]

NOTES

1. Clare Williams, trans., *Thomas Platter's Travels in England, 1599* (London: Jonathan Cape, 1937), p. 166. Williams translates Platter's journal from the German original and also describes the life and times of this indefatigable traveler and journal keeper.

2. See the *Oxford English Dictionary*, "Caesar," definition 1. The *OED* refers to Julius Caesar as a "dictator." Additional confusion on this point stems from the fact that the word "emperor" is derived from "imperator," a military term applied to a victorious commander in chief. Julius Caesar had been officially saluted as "imperator," and the word is stamped on many of the coins that bear his image. See John Dickinson, *Death of a Republic: Politics and Political Thought at Rome 59–44 B.C.* (New York: Macmillan, 1963), pp. 355–356.

3. Williams, *Platter's Travels*, pp. 166–167.

4. Ann Jennalie Cook, *The Privileged Playgoers of Shakespeare's London, 1576–1642* (Princeton, N.J.: Princeton University Press, 1981).

5. Andrew Gurr, *Playgoing in Shakespeare's London* (Cambridge: Cambridge University Press, 1987).

6. Scholars agree that 1599 is the most likely date for *Julius Caesar*'s earliest performances. Platter's journal, along with allusions in various other literary works, tells us the play could not have opened later. *Julius Caesar* is not included in a list of Shakespeare's plays given by Francis Meres in his *Palladis Tamia* of 1598, so presumably it had not been written at that date. This part of the evidence is a bit wobbly; Meres had not necessarily set out to make an exhaustive list, and he omitted some of Shakespeare's plays that had definitely been performed before 1598. Nevertheless, according to Marvin Spevack, editor of the New Cambridge Shakespeare's *Julius Caesar*, "scholars seem determined to have 1599 as the year in which *Julius Caesar* was written. There is no reason to disagree" (p. 6).

7. See J. B. Black, *The Reign of Elizabeth, 1558–1603*, 2nd ed. (Oxford: Clarendon Press, 1959, 1965), pp. 166–170.

8. Matthias Gelzer, *Caesar: Politician and Statesman*, trans. Peter Needham (Cambridge, Mass.: Harvard University Press, 1968), p. 324. The number of senators was amaz-

ingly large, around nine hundred (p. 310). Many had been appointed by Caesar within the past few years.

9. Gerard Walter, *Caesar: A Biography*, trans. Emma Craufurd (New York: Scribner's, 1952), p. 532. Historians have reported various activities during the interval after Caesar's death. Elizabeth H. Rawson has observed that "the precise course of events in the next few days is hard to reconstruct." See *The Cambridge Ancient History*, ed. J. A. Crook, Andrew Lintot, and Rawson, 2nd ed. (Cambridge: Cambridge University Press, 1982), vol. 9, p. 468.

10. Michael Grant, *Julius Caesar* (New York: M. Evans and Co., 1969, 1992), p. 157.

11. Frank Burr Marsh, *A History of the Roman World from 146 to 30 B.C.*, 3rd ed. (London: Methuen, 1963), p. 252.

12. Walter, *Caesar*, p. 534. Walter's book has fictional overtones, especially in his lavish provision of dialogue for all occasions, but he does follow recognized sources.

13. According to Walter, ibid., pp. 538–540, the question of Caesar's funeral was debated at a second Senate meeting on March 17, and the date of the funeral was set for several days later, probably March 20.

14. Robert S. Miola has reviewed the philosophical positions current in Shakespeare's day on the question of whether a tyrant might or might not justly be removed by assassination. See "*Julius Caesar* and the Tyrannicide Debate," *RenQ* 38 (1985), 271–289.

15. For a thorough investigation of Elizabethan schoolroom reading, see T. W. Baldwin, *William Shakspere's Small Latine & Less Greeke*, 2 vols. (Urbana, Ill.: University of Illinois Press, 1944). Baldwin's title, complete with esoteric spelling, is a quotation from a statement by Ben Jonson about his rival playwright's formal education; it does not represent Baldwin's personal opinion. Gilbert Highet's *The Classical Tradition: Greek and Roman Influences on Western Literature* (Oxford: Oxford University Press, 1949, 1957) surveys the subject from a wide perspective and discusses influences on Shakespeare in chapter 11 (pp. 194–218). Russ McDonald gives a useful guide to Shakespeare's reading in *The Bedford Companion to Shakespeare: An Introduction with Documents* (New York and Boston: Bedford Books of St. Martin's Press, 1996), pp. 100–117.

16. Albert Curtis Clark gives this translation from Cicero's *Familiar Letters*, 6.15, in "Cicero," *Encyclopedia Britannica*, 11th ed. (1910).

17. From Arthur Golding's 1567 translation of the *Metamorphoses*, ed. W.H.D. Rouse (Carbondale, Ill.: Southern Illinois University Press, 1961), p. 313. I have modernized the spelling. Shakespeare probably read the original Latin at school, but scholars have found enough direct verbal echoes to demonstrate that while writing his plays and poems, he kept Golding's translation at hand for reference. Golding's heptameter rhythm, though maddening to modern ears, is typical of much sixteenth-century verse.

18. See John W. Velz, "Clemency, Will, and Just Cause in *Julius Caesar*," *ShS* 22 (1969), 109–118. For Ovid, see p. 110.

19. See Rawson, *Cambridge Ancient History*, vol. 9, p. 475.

20. Francis Fergusson, *Trope and Allegory: Themes Common to Dante and Shakespeare* (Athens: University of Georgia Press, 1977), p. 1.

21. Quoted in *The Bedford Companion to Shakespeare*, p. 122. I have modernized the spelling.

22. Appian of Alexandria, who lived in the second century A.D. and wrote a history of Rome, is one of these possible sources. See Geoffrey Bullough, *Narrative and Dramatic Sources of Shakespeare* (London: Routledge and Kegan Paul, 1964), vol. 5, pp. 14–15, 156–159. See also Ernest Schanzer, *Shakespeare's Appian* (Liverpool: Liverpool University

Press, 1956). Another candidate is Suetonius, also of the second century A.D., whose *Lives of the Caesars* is known for its gossipy style. See Bullough, *Narrative*, p. 14. Suetonius, incidentally, repeats a rumor to the effect that Brutus was Caesar's illegitimate son. Shakespeare ignores this rumor in *Julius Caesar*.

23. These plays include Thomas Kyd's *Cornelia*, based on a play by the French tragic dramatist Robert Garnier, and the anonymous *Tragedy of Caesar and Pompey, or, Caesar's Revenge*, which was acted, presumably during the 1590s, at Trinity College, Oxford. A summary and excerpts from the latter work may be found in Bullough, *Narrative*, pp. 196–211.

24. Bullough, *Narrative*, p. 13, quoting Plutarch's *Life of Alexander*. I have modernized the spelling.

25. North's translation in its entirety has been edited by G. Wyndham (London: David North, 1895), 6 vols., for the Tudor Translations series; repr. 1967 for AMS Press, New York. Several editors have assembled the lives used by Shakespeare: *Julius Caesar, Marcus Brutus, Marcus Antonius,* and *Coriolanus.* Quotations from Plutarch in this book are taken from *Shakespeare's Plutarch*, ed. T.J.B. Spencer (Harmondsworth: Penguin, 1964), which uses modernized spelling. Page citations from Spencer's edition will be given parenthetically in my text. Excerpts from Plutarch related to *Julius Caesar* can be found in Bullough, *Narrative*, pp. 58–140 (in the original spelling) and also in many editions of the play.

26. Highet, *Classical Tradition*, p. 117.

27. Marvin Spevack, ed., *Julius Caesar* (Cambridge: Cambridge University Press, 1988), p. 11.

28. Harley Granville-Barker, *Prefaces to Shakespeare: Julius Caesar* (London and Portsmouth, N.H.: Heinemann, 1995 [1925]), p. 66.

3

DRAMATIC STRUCTURE

This chapter considers plot, characters, and language, although these large categories will be narrowed down a bit as we get into them. With regard to plot, we will examine the sequence of events in *Julius Caesar*'s five acts, with an eye to the suspense that carries from one scene to the next. This movement is particularly noticeable in *Julius Caesar* because the play has no subplots; everything that happens is directly related to the strong current of the main action. Character development in *Julius Caesar* is built to a large extent on patterns of tension and ambiguity. Finally, the discussion of language will focus particularly on the play's use of rhetoric, a major concern in a story that so often hinges on persuasion.

THE FIVE-ACT STRUCTURE

Julius Caesar and the Traditional Five Parts of Tragedy

Gustav Freytag, a nineteenth-century German novelist and critic, described the five phases of a traditionally structured tragedy in a way that has stuck in the critical mind and will be used here as we follow the events in *Julius Caesar*.[1] This sequence, sometimes called "Freytag's Pyramid," because it can be arranged as a triangular diagram, consists of the exposition, the rising action, the turning point (or climax), the falling action, and the ending, or the conclusion (or catastrophe). The terminology used by English-speaking critics may vary from one source to another.

Freytag, like literary critics before and since, was simply describing the patterns he had perceived in works of art that already existed. He was not issuing a set of instructions for writers of tragedy. Writers then and now derive their sense of structure from their familiarity with the tradition in which they are writing. Shakespeare, for example, knew the work of his own contemporaries and also of such contemporary dramatists as Seneca and Plautus.

Julius Caesar is divided into five acts in the play's only authentic text, the First Folio of 1623. Publishers were accustomed to setting up dramatic texts in this way. However, it is doubtful if actual playgoers were conscious of these formal divisions. Both the publisher's act divisions and Freytag's labels should be seen simply as conveniences, place markers to help us analyze an artistic work that would affect its audience in the same way whether these divisions and labels exist or not. In the case of *Julius Caesar*, the act division and Freytag's labels are at odds at one point. Ordinarily one expects Freytag's five parts to align themselves with the five act divisions. However, the printer who set up the divisions in *Julius Caesar* apparently paid more attention to making the acts of similar lengths than to following the internal logic of the play's construction, and as a result the exposition ends and the rising action begins while we are still in Act I.

The Exposition: Act I.i–ii

The opening of a play, the *exposition*, gives the audience the basic facts. We learn the setting in time and place, begin to learn about the main characters (whether or not we actually meet them at this early point), and get an idea of the conflict to be developed as the action proceeds. In *Julius Caesar* the exposition can be seen as occupying the first two scenes of Act I.

The exposition in this case is assisted by the play's title. The audience assumes it will find itself in ancient Rome, concerned with the man who in his time was the most powerful figure in the world. The audience also knows from history what will happen to him, and by whose hands. For the precise unfolding of events, however, we are on our own.

The play opens as the two tribunes, Flavius and Murellus, harangue a crowd of Roman commoners. The dialogue enables us to put together the situation. Rome is observing the traditional feast of the Lupercal, combined on this occasion with a triumphal celebration in honor of Caesar, who has defeated the sons of Pompey at the battle of Munda, in Spain. The implications give a hint of the conflict to come. The tribunes are angry because the crowd has forgotten its former admiration of Pompey and also because Caesar is celebrating a victory not over some foreign foe but over a faction of his fellow Romans. Public acclamation, we see, is fickle; one can be greeted with cheers one day and hisses the next. This fickleness will be an important factor as the play continues. The mention of Pompey also reminds us that Rome has been embroiled in civil strife, that bitterness and hatred still persist, and that Julius Caesar is not universally esteemed.

In I.ii, the exposition becomes more precise. We meet the main characters, see them in action, and are given assessments of their personalities. Cassius begins his carefully plotted seduction of Brutus into the conspiracy to assassinate Caesar; this undertaking is in itself a major piece of exposition, as from it we learn not only of Caesar's rise but of Cassius's and Brutus's reaction to it.

The exposition introduces not only the names of the major characters, but their public and private images, as seen by others and by themselves. As part of his manipulation, Cassius explains to Brutus what an honorable, courageous, and just person he, Brutus, is; Brutus heartily agrees. The audience is at liberty to accept this evaluation as it stands or to add a few grains of salt. We also notice Caesar's trustful friendship with Antony and hear his opinion of Cassius:

> Yond Cassius has a lean and hungry look,
> He thinks too much; such men are dangerous.   (194–195)

Caesar contrasts Cassius with Antony, who likes music and the theater and who, one assumes, in Caesar's opinion thinks just enough and not too much.

The ongoing action of I.ii also points toward future events. Casca tells Brutus and Cassius of Caesar's having been offered a crown; this episode pushes Brutus that much closer to his eventual role of assassin. And at the beginning of the scene, the Soothsayer sets up historical reverberations as he warns Caesar to beware the Ides of March. The audience can only look ahead.

Rising Action: Act I.iii through Act II

The *rising action* is sometimes called the complication, implying that we have now been supplied with enough data for the various components to start intertwining, building on the original situation, forming new patterns, and pushing the action toward the play's turning point. We see this happening in I.iii.

Some time has passed. The feast of the Lupercal was celebrated in February, and it is now close upon the fated Ides of March—the fifteenth of March. What most strikingly marks the transition to a new phase, however, is the storm—violent, energetic, and crowded with portents. Linked with the storm, emotionally and symbolically, is the conspiracy, which develops and comes to a head during this part of the play. Cassius has already done a great deal of groundwork. His conversations in this scene, first with Casca and then with Cinna, indicate that he has rounded up his group of potential assassins but has spoken with them only as individuals; the various members are now finding out one another's identity and forming a cohesive body.

The scene ends on two notes of suspense. The group will shortly be meeting for the first time as such: "Repair to Pompey's Porch, where you shall find us," Cassius tells Cinna (I.iii.147). One wonders how the meeting will go. A second point, of crucial importance to the conspirators, is their effort to enlist Brutus in the cause. As Cassius says to Casca, shrewdly giving Casca credit for thinking of a point the audience knows has been on Cassius's mind all along:

> Him and his worth, and our great need of him,
> You have right well conceited.   (151–152)

The rising action continues without a break in II.i. No time has passed, although the location has shifted. We find ourselves in Brutus's residence—specifically, according to many editions, in his orchard; the scene is sometimes called the "or-chard scene." Here we share Brutus's thoughts in a soliloquy. He has already made up his mind that Caesar must be killed. This decision takes care of one of the bits of suspense with which the previous scene ended; the other, our curiosity about the conspirators' meeting, is resolved shortly afterward. The conspirators call upon Brutus, are introduced one by one to him and thus to the audience—an efficient device on Shakespeare's part—and the meeting continues, having added Brutus as a new member. What then happens is that Brutus takes over. He reverses Cassius's suggestions, moves into Cassius's role as recruiter when Casca proposes sounding out Caius Ligarius, and dismisses the group with a pep talk: "Good gentlemen, look fresh and merrily" (224).

Having dealt with the suspense with which it opened, this same scene creates some new suspense to exert a pull on the audience. Now we wonder what will become of the conspiracy with Brutus at its head. Another pressing question, which has worried the group, is whether Caesar will come to the Capitol the next morning and thus make himself accessible to his killers. Decius Brutus, one of the conspirators we have just met, has boasted of his ability to talk Caesar into anything, but one never knows. Something might intervene. A third question, ominous indeed, is that of secrecy and betrayal. How many people know of the plot, and can they be trusted? Portia's dialogue with Brutus, after the main body of conspirators leaves the house, turns on this fear of an intelligence leak. Portia has to assure her husband that she is trustworthy and would not reveal his secret under any circumstances. Finally, the scene's closing lines return to the question of Brutus as leader. Caius Ligarius enters and declares himself an enthusiastic convert:

> . . . I follow you,
> To do I know not what; but it sufficeth
> That Brutus leads me on.   (331–334)

Brutus replies, "Follow me, then." The stage direction, from the original First Folio text, adds, "*Thunder.*"

The following scene (II.ii) is filled with irony, for the audience knows more than many of the characters onstage. We are in Julius Caesar's house, and we see the morning of March 15 from his viewpoint. The storm has brought bad dreams to Calphurnia and indecision to Caesar; he wavers between refusing her request that he stay home and yielding to it. But Decius Brutus enters and fulfills his earlier boast, reinterpreting Calphurnia's dream as a lucky omen and persuading Caesar to go to the Capitol. A number of conspirators then enter, along with two visitors who are not in on the plot: Antony and the aged senator Publius. On the surface, the gathering is friendly, even festive. Beneath the surface, suspense tightens. Curiously, this effect holds despite the fact that we know from history, just as Shakespeare's original audience did, that Caesar will in fact be killed. The play's moment-by-moment immediacy, its constant flow as one event leads into another, makes it easy to immerse ourselves in it.

Scenes iii and iv of Act II continue this suspense, focusing on the danger of discovery. Certainly Artemidorus, whose letter to Caesar comprises the whole of scene iii, knows all about the plot, including the names of the plotters, and has every intention of passing this information along to Caesar. Artemidorus does not tell us where he got his facts. For the sake of suspense, all we need to know is that there has been a leak somewhere.

The Soothsayer, who appears in scene iv, also knows that Caesar is in danger. Presumably his knowledge results from supernatural intuition rather than actual evidence. Asked if he knows of any harm intended toward Caesar, he replies, "None that I know will be, much that I fear may chance" (33). Portia, who has asked the question and has come out into the street in an agony of fear that the plot might fail, is all the more terrified. Brutus has told her his secret, as she had begged him to do. Now all she can do is wait.

Turning Point: Act III

The precise identification of a play's *turning point* is often a matter of debate. In *Julius Caesar*, we might nominate several such points. Caesar's murder, after which the conspirators cannot change their minds and decide not to do it after all, and Antony's speech to the Roman crowd, after which events take a turn the conspirators had not predicted, are clear candidates. Another possible turning point, located between these two, is the entrance of Antony's servant shortly after Caesar has been murdered (III.i.121), announcing his master's intention to appear in person. Several critics have felt that it is this moment that swings the play around and heads it in a different direction.[2]

The action of the previous scene continues in III.i, no lapse of time having occurred. Caesar is still on the way to the Capitol, attended by his supposed friends. The Soothsayer and Artemidorus try unsuccessfully to get Caesar's attention. A hint of danger, a final tightening of suspense, comes with the greeting Popilius Lena gives Cassius, "I wish your enterprise today may thrive" (13). Despite Cassius's sudden panic—"I fear our purpose is discovered"—Popilius Lena does not betray the conspirators.

The killing itself is very brief as far as the text is concerned, although in performance it is sometimes done at length and even in slow motion. The conspirators gather around Caesar, pretending to plead a cause; then, with Casca giving the word—"Speak, hands, for me"—the deed is done. "They stab Caesar," says the stage direction in the First Folio. Usually when the scene is acted, Brutus is the last to strike. In some productions the wounded Caesar has turned to Brutus for help before realizing that he too is a traitor: "*Et tu, Brute.*"

It is at this point that the suspense seems suddenly to end. This impression is temporary, for the strings will soon tighten again, and we will be drawn along. But there is a pause. Julius Caesar is dead, and the world is a different place. The conspirators catch their breaths, bathe their hands in Caesar's blood, speculate on the fame they and their action will acquire in the future, and plan their next step, to walk out into the marketplace waving their bloody swords.

Suspense now returns to the play in the person of Mark Antony. The conspirators thought they had accounted for him. In planning the assassination, they had assigned Trebonius the job of drawing Antony aside, out of the Senate chamber altogether, lest he impulsively try to defend his friend. But they did not perceive Antony as much of a threat in any case. Cassius had earlier suggested he be killed along with Caesar (II.i.155–161), but Brutus had disapproved. Antony, Brutus claimed, would be powerless without Caesar and, moreover, is given "to sports, to wildness, and much company" (189). He would be incapable of serious action, in other words. Trebonius had then chimed in:

> There is no fear in him; let him not die,
> For he will live, and laugh at this hereafter.   (190–191)

The irony in these lines has now come back to haunt the conspirators.

Antony proceeds to take over the action. Brutus had told his colleagues to bathe their hands in Caesar's blood; Antony now shakes these bloody hands, systematically, calling out the assassins' names as if he were standing in some grisly receiving line. Paradoxically, Antony dominates Brutus by taking advantage of Brutus's determination to appear calm and in control. When Antony asks permission to speak at Caesar's funeral, Brutus at once agrees, possibly to conceal the fact that he has not given a thought to Caesar's funeral, and he calms Cassius's fears at this unexpected development. He, Brutus, will explain to the people that Antony speaks only "by leave and by permission," and that will make everything all right.

At the end of the scene, the conspirators leave the stage, and Antony, as if to demonstrate his new power, holds onto the spotlight for a soliloquy. The purpose he expresses is that of revenging Caesar's murder; the means, those of chaos and violence—but a violence, we begin to realize, controlled by Antony's manipulative skill. The play has gained a new focus of suspense, and we look forward to finding out what Antony will do next.

Brutus's and Antony's respective speeches (III.ii) will be analyzed for rhetorical effect later in this chapter. With regard to the plot, we are particularly aware of the sequence. Brutus's brisk message reflects the speaker's inability to imagine anyone disagreeing with him, so that he states what he assumes will serve as a sufficient justification for his action and then departs. He thinks he has closed the chapter. Ironically, he has merely provided an introduction.

Antony's skill at orchestrating the crowd provides the second-phase turning point. At the end of his speech, while the mob howls for vengeance and Brutus and Cassius are reported to have fled from Rome, the audience knows that the play has moved irrevocably into another phase.

First, though, the events of Act III restate themselves in a kind of coda. Cinna the Poet's death (III.iii) does not further the plot and may seem a gratuitous addition, but it provides a link between past and future. The "dogs of war" so enthusiastically invoked by Antony (III.i.273) do not necessarily choose their victims according to ideologies of justice, and Cinna dies simply because the mob wants to kill somebody.

The Falling Action: Act IV

Typically, the *falling action* phase of a tragedy brings a sense of gathering momentum. Events hasten toward their inevitable end. At the same time, the play provides some surprises; not everything can be predicted. In Act IV of *Julius Caesar*, we know that Brutus and Cassius will be defeated, yet we find ourselves surprised by the pattern of parallel disintegration that sets in on both sides of the struggle, cleaving both sets of allies.

The rivalry between Antony and Octavius Caesar, Julius Caesar's grand-nephew and adopted heir, is a surprise to the audience (assuming, of course, that the audience has suspended its prior historical knowledge and entered into the world of the play) because Octavius had not even been mentioned prior to III.i.279, when Antony receives a message from him. Now, in the first scene of Act IV and the beginning of the play's falling action, Antony and Octavius are in Rome, uneasily sharing power. Their antagonism is subtly expressed at this point. Antony describes the third member of the triumvir, Lepidus, as a "slight, unmeritable man" (12) and hints that he, Antony, and Octavius combine to push Lepidus out. Octavius quietly declines the offer and stands up for Lepidus.

The quarrel between Brutus and Cassius (IV.ii, iii) is similar to Antony's and Octavius's mutual distrust in that it shows a partnership under stress, but it becomes a strong contrast in the emotional heat engendered. Here in Sardis (now in modern Turkey), Cassius and Brutus brace themselves for the showdown they know will come. External circumstance has put them under great pressure; anger, accusations, and mutual blame not unnaturally result. Despite the reconciliation that eventually takes place, the audience feels that the conspirators are on a downhill slide. When Caesar's ghost appears to Brutus and announces his control of the future—"thou shalt see me at Philippi" (iii.284)—the sense of inevitability grows stronger.

The Conclusion: Act V

The final phase of a play has been denoted by a variety of terms. "Catastrophe," a traditional label, has picked up misleading connotations for modern readers, reminding us of disaster films or other manifestations of sudden and large-scale misfortune. Another possibility, "denouement," literally means the action of untying, as of a knot, and can be appropriate to plays that rely upon revelations of fact—the identity of a foundling child, for example—to shape up the plot at the end. However, since *Julius Caesar* does not go in for this sort of surprise, it seems simplest to refer to the ending as the *conclusion*.

The straightforward pattern of *Julius Caesar*'s conclusion gives it a ritual quality. We know what will happen; indeed, the participants themselves know what will happen; and it happens. The battle opens with a taunting ceremony between the opposing sides (V.i.21–66), followed by the solemn farewell of Brutus to Cassius:

> If we do meet again, why, we shall smile;
> If not, why then this parting was well made.   (117–118)

Later, Brutus even mentions Caesar's ghost, which has kept its promise:

> The ghost of Caesar hath appear'd to me
> Two several times by night; at Sardis once,
> And this last night, here in Philippi fields.
> I know my hour is come.   (V.v.17–19)

The battle is portrayed by means of a familiar Shakespearean technique, as a series of short scenes, giving an impression of numerous actions spread over a large and confusing territory. Much of the dialogue transmits information about what is happening elsewhere. This hurry and scurry serves as a matrix for the trio of suicides—Cassius's, Titinius's, and Brutus's—which bring the action to a close.

Aristotle has written that a tragedy should depict a complete action.[3] Surely this is the case in *Julius Caesar*. The audience feels at the close of the play that an era has definitely ended. The hint of the new era about to begin comes strongly through in the play's closing lines as Octavius, whose mood is naturally upbeat at this point, refers to the battle just past as "this happy day."

CHARACTER DEVELOPMENT

The term *character development* may be read in two ways, and both will be taken into account in this discussion. In one sense, the characters themselves develop, or perhaps fail to develop, during the course of the play. It might be argued, for example, that in many cases it is not the characters who change but their circumstances, and that the characters simply respond to these changes. In another sense, the playwright develops his characters by allowing the audience to find out more and more about them.

This latter sense of development progresses by several routes. The audience sees the characters in action, listens to their dialogue, and sometimes enters their thoughts by means of a soliloquy. Further evidence is provided by the characters' descriptions of one another. None of these perspectives can be taken as absolute. Shakespeare creates characters who are perfectly capable of misjudging their fellow characters, of deliberately deceiving others or unconsciously deceiving themselves.

Both major and minor characters in *Julius Caesar* can be multifaceted and often ambiguous.[4] How is an individual character to be interpreted? Is he a good person or a bad person? Who is the central character in the play? Which is the leading role? (Julius Caesar himself, Brutus, and Antony have been suggested.) Or is there a leading role at all, rather than a pattern of different personalities, an ensemble effect?

Leah Scragg supports this last possibility:

> The focus of attention in *Julius Caesar* shifts from act to act, with the character to whom the members of the audience relate in one scene being distanced

from them in the next. The play thus affords the spectator a variety of perspectives upon the situation, rather than exploring a single experience, and involves the theater audience in a constant process of revaluation as the focal point of the action shifts.[5]

Julius Caesar

The nomination of Julius Caesar himself for the play's leading role has in its favor the fact that the play is named for him and also that he is one of history's most prominent figures. Unfortunately, Caesar's death halfway through the play casts a cloud on his candidacy, and actors who otherwise would line up to audition for the role may well have second thoughts. A leading character, a protagonist, should, one somehow feels, carry on to the end and hold the audience's attention throughout, even if a tragic death awaits him in the final scene.

From a more theoretical standpoint, Caesar can be seen as dominating the play, even after his death. He does return as a ghost (IV.iii.274–287), to speak ominous words to Brutus. Further, his name is invoked by his assassins during the final battle, when things are going badly for them: "O Julius Caesar, thou art mighty yet" (V.iii.94).

Whether regarded as the central character or an important piece in an ensemble, Shakespeare's Julius Caesar can be seen from a variety of angles, many of them controversial. Is he an ambitious tyrant, moving inexorably toward total political domination, as Brutus decides to see him? And if so, if Caesar does indeed aim to consolidate control of the Roman world permanently into his own hands, does this totalitarian goal proceed from a patriotic concern for the good of his country or from his own personal greed? He has already named an heir, Octavius, but does this action show that he is willing to share power? Or is Octavius basically an insurance policy, to inherit a place of authority only upon Caesar's death?

Aside from Caesar's plans for the future—to become king or not to become king, and, if so, what kind of king—readers and audiences are faced with numerous reactions to Caesar as a personality. Would we enjoy Caesar's company? Probably we would not, as Shakespeare has given him lines that convey an arrogant concern with his own superiority. He rejects ordinary human frailties, remarking to Antony that "I rather tell thee what is to be fear'd / Than what I fear; for always I am Caesar" (I.ii.211–212). (A moment later, however, he admits to being deaf in his left ear.) Along the same lines of invulnerability, Caesar defies danger:

> . . . The things that threaten'd me
> Ne'er looked but on my back; when they shall see
> The face of Caesar, they are vanished.   (II.ii.10–12)

Caesar is, or thinks he is, unshakable in his opinions and thus above everyone else: "I could be well mov'd, if I were as you" (III.i.58).

But is Caesar's arrogance a criminal offense? The world is full of pompous people. And might not Caesar have some understandable reason for his self-inflation?

Today we are tolerant of, or at least not automatically infuriated by, politicians who try to maintain a public image verging on the superhuman. This trait seems to come with the territory. Moreover, Caesar displays hospitality to his friends and a sense of duty to the public. Fatally, he refuses to read Artemidorus's letter because, having been told it concerns him closely, he replies, "What touches us ourself shall be last serv'd" (III.i.8).

Shakespeare's display of Caesar's weaknesses need not necessarily add up to a weak or trivial character. The opposite might even be the case. Alexander Leggatt suggests that these weaknesses might be seen as irrelevant:

> Shakespeare's Caesar is a convincing portrait of a great man seen in private. A little reading of history shows that men of genius who make this kind of impact are generally not modest, healthy, balanced, and reasonable people. They can be maddening, monstrous, and pathetic, as Caesar is. Their private lives and medical records do not bear examination. If Shakespeare goes daringly far in showing this aspect of Caesar the man, it may be because he wants to emphasize that his greatness consists not so much in what he says or does as in the mysterious impact he has on others.[6]

The audience's judgment of Caesar affects the play's whole pattern of characterization. An innocent Caesar, one who simply wants the best for his country or who at least is guilty of no crime deserving death, makes Cassius and Brutus appear the more villainous. On the other hand, if he is seen as a potential, if not quite actual, tyrant, one who will brook no opposition politically or personally and who promises to become even more unbending as time goes on, then Cassius and Brutus might have more grounds for audience sympathy. The play gives us many choices.

Brutus

To many readers and audiences, past and present, Brutus is the prime candidate for the play's central character. It is possible to see him as a tragic hero, possessed of a fatal flaw in the shape of excessive idealism. Brutus is onstage for much of the action, and he does not disappear from the audience's awareness even when he is off. He dies at the correct time for a hero—just at the end. Other characters constantly express their admiration of him. Moreover, Brutus has an interior life. We are admitted into his mind, presumably into his truest conscious thoughts, as he speaks to himself or to his friends and followers.

Not surprisingly in view of these attributes, leading actors from the seventeenth century onward have seen Brutus as a heroic protagonist and have taken the part for themselves. For much of the play's critical history, critics have also approved of Brutus, though sometimes with reservations. David Bevington, for example, feels that although "the conspiracy founders on Brutus's repeated insistence on having his way," nevertheless "Brutus's fatal limitations as leader of a coup d'etat are inseparable from his virtues as a private man. The truth is that such a noble man is, by his very nature, unsuited for the stern exigencies of assassination and civil war."[7]

Geoffrey Miles has suggested that Brutus's real self was corrupted by Cassius, who substituted a tyrannical self-image for Brutus to adopt. Brutus did not realize a substitution had taken place. "This failure in self-knowledge of the play's most introspective character is symptomatic of a world in which people see their actions most clearly as reflected in the eyes of others."[8]

Some readers have been so predisposed to find Brutus a thoroughly noble character that they go to energetic lengths to evade the more ambiguous evidence supplied by the text. Harley Granville-Barker, for example, is troubled by the textual tangle in IV.iii, in which Brutus first tells Cassius about Portia's death and then, on hearing the news from Messala, gives the impression that he did not already know it and reacts with impressive calm (181–193). Granville-Barker suggests, as many other critics have done, that Shakespeare intended but forgot to cut one or the other of these passages, or perhaps did cut one of them, only to have it restored inadvertently. But Granville-Barker cannot seem to stop himself from suspecting that perhaps Shakespeare did intend for both passages to stand. To negate the distressing implications of a calculating and impression-managing Brutus, Granville-Barker invents a hypothesis that presents Shakespeare as remarkably opaque about his own work:

> He [Shakespeare] may have thought there was now a double effect to be gained (the original one had not been perhaps so bad, it had only not been good enough); and, in performance, there is an arbitrary sort of effect in the passage as it stands. It is quite likely that, patching at the thing, he did not see to what subtle reflections upon Brutus's character the new combination would give rise (so seldom apparently did he consider the troubles of his future editors!). I hope that he made the cut. I think on the whole that he did. I am sure that he should have done, and I recommend the producer [director] of today to make it, and by no means to involve his Brutus in that incidental lie, nor his character in the even more objectionable subtleties of an escape from it.[9]

The advancing decades of the twentieth century have seen the spread of numerous cracks in Brutus's noble image. E.A.J. Honigman has analyzed these systematically, comparing Plutarch's and Shakespeare's respective Brutuses and finding that Shakespeare's character "differs from Plutarch's Marcus Brutus in making many more political mistakes, in muddling his arguments, and in thinking too well of himself."[10] Today's readers and audiences appear more alert to irony and paradox, more willing to suspect the existence of a flimsy facade and to try to see through it, than seems to be the case in previous generations. Brutus's behavior when he meets with the conspirators (II.i.86–228), for example, and immediately starts issuing orders, rebuffing his associates, and allowing no argument with his pronouncements, behaving in fact very much like Caesar himself, is immediately noticeable to today's theater audiences. It is true, of course, that the audience may pick up this message because actors deliberately send it out. We are all in the age of irony together.

Brutus's decisions are not only peremptory but frequently wrong, from the standpoint of practical success. He advises against killing Mark Antony (II.i.162ff.);

later, he gives Antony permission to speak at Caesar's funeral (III.i.231); then, after he and Cassius have fled from Rome, he insists on meeting Caesar's troops at Philippi instead of waiting for the enemy to come to them (IV.iii.213)—a disastrous strategy. Brutus's words on this last occasion have so noble a resonance that they are often quoted out of context by editorial writers and motivational speakers, as an incentive to immediate action:

> There is a tide in the affairs of men
> Which, taken at the flood, leads on to fortune;
> Omitted, all the voyage of their life
> Is bound in shallows and in miseries.   (IV.iii.217–221)

Perhaps it is this noble resonance that intensifies today's readers' suspicions about Brutus, just as this same resonance assured previous generations that Brutus was indeed everything he and his other admirers thought he was.

At the same time, however, it would hardly be fair to accuse Brutus of setting out intentionally to deceive, to construct a persona and then foist it on the public. To many readers and audiences, Brutus is a compelling case of self-deception. He longs to be noble, pure, objective, and untainted by personal greed; he consequently declares himself to be this person, with enough conviction to sway those of his friends who, conveniently, want to have a noble person in their lives even though they feel that they themselves are not quite up to the role. In responding to Cassius's initial overtures, for example, Brutus declares a personal manifesto:

> What is it that you would impart to me?
> If it be ought toward the general good,
> Set honor in one eye and death in th' other,
> And I will look on both indifferently;
> For let the gods so speed me as I love
> The name of honor more than I fear death.   (I.ii.84–89)

It is true that Brutus sometimes fills his self-designed role with some credit. He speaks kindly to his young servant Lucius (II.i.39; IV.iii.255–266). In his conversation with Portia, he is courteous, loving, and apparently quite sincere (II.i.234–309). These interpersonal transactions, however, are fairly simple ones. In a more complex situation, Brutus appears unable to survey a range of options, compare them, and choose the best. Instead he leaps to some simple and ideologically appealing stance, whether or not it fits the circumstances or even, when viewed objectively, retains any ethical justification.

Brutus's quarrel with Cassius in Act IV, for example, is based partly on the fact that Brutus needs to pay his soldiers and Cassius has not sent him money to do so. Brutus himself has no funds, as he angrily tells Cassius, because "I can raise no money by vile means" (iii.71)—by oppressing the local population, he means. The soldiers nevertheless must be paid. Brutus's solution is to demand that Cassius raise the money, by vile means presumably, so that he himself can keep his hands clean.

Thus, it is possible to view Brutus as a self-deceived poseur. And yet this label too is unsatisfactory. Are we to give no credit to good intentions, noble ideals? Should decisions be judged solely by the results? Brutus at least tries to be honorable, to set high standards for himself. Should he be condemned because his ideals came to a bad end? Perhaps the answer is yes; a little nobility is a dangerous thing. Nevertheless, Brutus's characterization retains the ambiguity so typical of this play. We cannot put him into some neat compartment and have done with it.

Antony

A third candidate for the protagonist of *Julius Caesar* is Mark Antony, even though, not surprisingly, the role may be viewed from conflicting angles.

As a character, Antony develops considerably during the progress of the play. In this he differs from Julius Caesar and Brutus, both of whom remain much the same, even though their circumstances undergo a drastic shift. Antony begins as merely a friend of Caesar, known for his love of merrymaking, hardly someone to take seriously. The conspirators misjudge him in this way; Antony is "but a limb of Caesar," according to Brutus (II.i.165). Consequently, the moment in which Shakespeare's Antony confronts the murdered corpse of Caesar (III.i.148ff.) might be seen as the crossroads of his life, or rather of his character development within this play.

But into what does Antony develop? While the assassins are present, Antony presents himself as a shocked and grieving mourner for Caesar, but one whose admiration for the killers—"the choice and master spirits of this age"—apparently prevents any thought of redress. That the conspirators would buy this protestation seems surprising, but, led by Brutus, they do. A few minutes later, when alone with Caesar's body, Antony implies that he has been wearing a temporary mask:

> O pardon me, thou bleeding piece of earth,
> That I am meek and gentle with these butchers.   (254–255)

Antony then invokes war and violence, "domestic fury and fierce civil strife," on behalf of "Caesar's spirit, ranging for revenge." (To "range" is to "rove in search of prey.")

These passages would seem to indicate that Antony has been converted, quite suddenly, from reveler to avenger. Such an assumption is satisfying from the standpoints of both character development and plot motivation. The conversion leads into Antony's next move—the funeral oration that brings the Roman mob first to tears and then to fury.

Revenge does not seem to have a direct bearing on Antony's actions after the conspirators flee the city. Grabbing power for himself was not part of the agenda he envisioned as he stood over the corpse of Caesar; at least, this ambition was not verbalized in his soliloquy. But in the first scene of Act IV, we see Antony with his fellow power sharers, Octavius Caesar and Lepidus, deciding which of their political opponents are to be put to death. Antony's heart, so warm in defense of Caesar, seems to have undergone a convenient icing over, even in regard to his own family. The triumvirs are bargaining among themselves. Lepidus consents to the death of his own brother, claiming in exchange the condemnation of Antony's nephew. Antony has no objection and even marks the list himself: "He shall not live; look, with a spot I damn him" (6).

This scene, the so-called proscription scene, marks Antony's low point in the audience's regard. He becomes a more likable character in the last act, possibly because he is now an underdog, helpless against the subtle opposition of Octavius.

Antony's eulogy over the body of Brutus (V.v.68–75) shows him in a good light as well. True, he may in this endeavor be less than completely sincere, since in earlier parts of the play he has exerted himself to show Brutus as anything but a noble Roman. But it is equally possible that Antony is yielding to an impulse of generosity. To see another person as that person sees himself can be a kind thing to do, a parting gift in this instance.

Cassius

Cassius is not a serious candidate for the play's leading character, but actors are eager to play him. His inner contradictions make him a challenge. He possesses a shrewd, objective common sense; he can see the bottom line. But he is also swayed by his passions. These include envy of Caesar and a deep need to be loved, especially by Brutus.

For his part, Caesar's opinion of Cassius is decidedly negative:

> Seldom he [Cassius] smiles, and smiles in such a sort
> As if he mock'd himself, and scorn'd his spirit
> That could be mov'd to smile at any thing.
> Such men as he be never at heart's ease
> Whiles they behold a greater than themselves,
> And therefore is he very dangerous.   (I.II.205–210)

Caesar's intuition is correct, as the audience already knows, having just seen Cassius at work luring Brutus into what will become a conspiracy to kill Caesar.

Cassius's attitude toward Brutus is complex. He genuinely admires him and seeks his approval. At the same time, he is not above exploiting him by underhanded means. Following his opening move in the temptation of Brutus, Cassius soliloquizes:

> Well, Brutus, thou art noble; yet I see
> Thy honorable mettle may be wrought
> From that it is dispos'd.   (I.ii.308–310)

Cassius then sends Brutus anonymous letters, purporting to be from Romans worried about Caesar's potential for tyranny, urging Brutus to take patriotic action.

Cassius (Julian Glover) watches as Brutus (John Nettles) ponders the danger of Caesar's ambition. Stratford-upon-Avon, 1995. Reproduced by courtesy of the Shakespeare Centre Library, Stratford-upon-Avon.

Cassius here seems to take pleasure in his skill at deception. He lets another of the conspirators, Cinna, in on the game by giving him the job of delivering the letters (I.iii.142–146). One wonders if Cassius's capacity for envy extends to Brutus himself, despite his paradoxical need for Brutus's affection. Knowing that he himself is unlikely to acquire a reputation for idealistic nobility, he sets out to manipulate and thus dominate someone who does have it.

As soon as Brutus joins the group, however, Cassius begins to crumple. Brutus consistently gets his own way, even when his way points to doom. This passivity seems linked to another of Cassius's traits: his urge toward, or fascination with, self-destruction. Suicide would seem to be Cassius's automatic response to any threat. Upon Casca's reference to Caesar's growing power, Cassius replies:

> I know where I will wear this dagger then;
> Cassius from bondage will deliver Cassius.   (I.iii.89–90)

Again, just before the assassination, when for a moment Cassius thinks the plot has been discovered, his reaction is similar:

> Brutus, what shall be done? If this be known,
> Cassius or Caesar never shall turn back,
> For I will slay myself.   (III.i.20–22)

On going into battle, Cassius checks to be sure Brutus is as ready as he himself to commit suicide if defeated. His earlier manipulative skills return to him on this occasion, for, although he finds that Brutus at first holds the wrong opinion on this matter, he is able to persuade him to a reversal (V.i.96–112).

It is ironically fitting that Cassius, so complex, so often at odds with himself, should finally die upon a misperception. Titinius, sent by Cassius to identify a nearby troop of horsemen on the battlefield, is seen surrounded by this troop; in actuality he has met a group of friends, but Cassius assumes he has been captured. To avoid his own capture, Cassius then arranges his death.

Minor Characters

Calphurnia and Portia

With the exception of Brutus's servant Lucius, who appears in both sections, minor characters in *Julius Caesar* work in two shifts, changing in Act IV. This arrangement facilitated the doubling of parts among Shakespeare's actors, as it often does in productions today.

The only women in the play, Portia and Calphurnia, appear in the first shift, in Act II. Their functions are parallel. Each is devoted to her husband and fears any danger that may threaten him. The fact that the husband of the one is plotting to kill the husband of the other gives an ironic emphasis to the wives' symmetry. Calphurnia has the aid of the supernatural in trying to prevent her husband's leaving the house on the Ides of March, since she has dreamed prophetically of blood and death, but she also relies on her own personality. She is not ordinarily superstitious, has "never stood on ceremonies" (II.ii.13), and this habit of common sense adds credibility to her alarm. Nevertheless, she does not succeed. Caesar, though he yields at first, changes his mind and goes forth.

Portia is at first more successful in that she does persuade Brutus to tell her his secret, but she is ultimately just as ineffective as Calphurnia. She cannot influence events or help Brutus when he flees from Rome. It could be argued that she harms him instead, since her despair and suicide (IV.iii.155–156) have a negative effect on Brutus's morale.

Innocent victims of violent events are necessary for the play's sense of magnitude; Caesar's assassination sends out wide ripples. Although we will encounter more innocent victims as we examine the characters, the two wives, balanced on either side of the play's opposition, have an effect much greater than their small number of lines would indicate.

The Conspirators

The largest single group of minor characters in the first three acts are the conspirators recruited by Cassius and Brutus, six in all, whom the audience gets to know to a greater or lesser degree.

Of these, Casca appears most frequently and has the most strongly delineated personality. This personality, however, may seem self-contradictory. His first line, calling for quiet so that Caesar can speak (I.ii.2), seems to show him as a devoted flunky, making his loyalty to Caesar as obvious as he can. Yet when he tells Brutus and Cassius of Antony's offering Brutus the crown (235–287), he takes a cynical, disillusioned tone, implying that Caesar really wanted the crown, even though he refused it. He gives a less than gracious reply to Cassius's dinner invitation: "Aye, if I be alive, and your mind hold, and your dinner worth the eating" (291–292), and Brutus is then prompted to call him a "blunt fellow."

This level-headed bluntness changes to almost hysterical fear when Casca next appears (I.iii), terrified by the storm and the supernatural portents that accompany it. Cassius talks Casca into a tougher mood, and Casca then goes to the conspirators' meeting and adds his voice to whatever sentiment prevails. Cicero, he says, echoing Cassius, should not be left out of the plot; but when Brutus objects, Casca swings around at once: "Indeed, he is not fit" (II.i.153). Later, Casca is the first to stab Caesar, apparently by prearrangement with his colleagues: "Speak, hands, for me" (III.i.76). He then disappears from the play.

Casca's seemingly fragmented personality might perhaps be unified from the audience's perspective if he is seen as an insecure person who will do whatever it takes to be accepted. The storm scene would then come nearest to his true self; fear is just beneath the surface in Casca. In this episode, he recovers his balance as soon as Cassius offers him a role to play, that of assassin. Casca becomes once again the "blunt fellow," brave and trustworthy, as he describes himself:

> You speak to Casca, and to such a one
> That is no fleering tell-tale. Hold, my hand.
> Be factious for redress of all these griefs,
> And I will set this foot of mine as far
> As who goes farthest.   (I.iii.116–119)

The historical Casca fled Rome after the assassination and took part in the battle of Philippi, where Plutarch describes him urging Brutus to kill some of his prisoners.[11] Other historians have included Casca among those who committed suicide after the battle, but Plutarch does not mention this final act.[12] Shakespeare may or may not have been aware of it. Casca's disappearance after Act III may have been a simple matter of practicality, if the actor who played him were needed for another role.

The other conspirators are less distinctly drawn. Cinna (not Cinna the Poet) has already become a trusted associate of Cassius by the time we meet him, in the last scene of Act I; he has apparently been instrumental in setting up a meeting at Pompey's Porch (I.iii.146–147). We meet the others in a lump, so to speak, when Cassius brings them to call on Brutus at the beginning of Act II. As the action continues, we come to know them by their deeds. Caius Ligarius, the last to join the conspiracy, gets up from his sickbed to rush to Brutus's house (II.i.310–334). Decius Brutus (to be distinguished from the major character Marcus Brutus) calls on Caesar the next morning and persuades him to go to the Capitol. Trebonius has the job of drawing Mark Antony out of the way before the assassination begins (III.i.25–26). Metellus Cimber is the brother of a man Caesar has banished, whose cause becomes the pretext for the conspirators to gather around Caesar when the moment approaches.

Tribunes and Senators

Among the nonconspiring minor characters are the two tribunes in the first scene, Flavius and Murellus (according to the spelling of the First Folio; in Plutarch we find Marullus). The tribunes at that time were magistrates chosen from among the plebians, or nonpatrician burgesses. Flavius and Murellus berate the crowd for their admiration of Caesar (I.i.32–60) and then pull the garlands off Caesar's statues. Later, in punishment, they are "put to silence" (ii.286), a most ominous phrase, but one that seems to have meant merely that they were deprived of their offices and thus lost their right to express an authoritative opinion. Flavius is later glimpsed at the battle of Philippi, although the First Folio's spelling obscures the situation; a "Flavio" is mentioned near the end of V.iii, and a moment later a "Flavius" enters. He (or they) have no lines. The historical character was not present at this battle.

Two nonconspiring senators, Popilius Lena and Publius, are part of the action surrounding Caesar's death. Popilius Lena's greeting to Cassius, "I wish your enterprise today may thrive" (III.i.12), is taken from Plutarch and serves the purpose of tightening the preassassination suspense. Publius, puzzling in some ways, is not mentioned in Plutarch. He calls on Caesar on the morning of the Ides of March, arriving at the same time as the conspirators (II.ii.107). Later, in the confusion following Caesar's murder, Brutus and Cassius reassure him and urge him to go away lest further commotion "should do your age some mischief" (III.i.93). His function may be to represent the innocent and horrified bystander, "quite confounded by this mutiny" (86). If Publius is an old man, as the line quoted above clearly indicates, he would hardly be the nephew of Antony to whose death Antony later consents (IV.i.4–5). Shakespeare invented both Publiuses, since historically Antony had no nephew by that name.

Cicero

Cicero's classification as a minor character in *Julius Caesar* stems from the fact that he appears only three times, two of these wordlessly, and in his conversation with Casca, in the midst of the storm, speaks a total of nine lines (I.iii.1–40). In history and in literature, Cicero is a towering figure. He was a public personage, a holder of important offices, and a poet and philosopher. He originated a clear and rhythmic Latin style that influenced the art of writing in his own and later languages. His letters and speeches have been studied through the centuries, in Shakespeare's time and our own.

In *Julius Caesar*, Cicero is more talked about than talking. He is glimpsed in processions, and he is present at the Lupercalian games when the crown is offered to Caesar, but Casca, describing this last event, cannot report Cicero's words because he does not understand the language: "It was Greek to me" (I.ii.284). Greek language and philosophy, in both of which Cicero was deeply interested, struck some Romans as an elitist affectation, and Casca would seem to be of this party. We can assume that Cicero's words on this occasion were not flattering to Caesar. Cicero had taken Pompey's side in the recent civil war and considered Caesar an enemy. Brutus, who does not like Cicero despite the fact that he does not like Caesar either, notes Cicero's demeanor as he returns from the games:

> . . . And Cicero
> Looks with such ferret and such fiery eyes
> As we have seen him in the Capitol,
> Being cross'd in conference by some senators.   (185–188)

As a Stoic, Cicero practiced detachment from the external world, a trait Shakespeare includes in his characterization. Casca, undone by the storm, finds it hard to believe that Cicero is frightened by neither natural violence nor supernatural portents, and tries to convince him that such things as fiery men walking the streets are a significant departure from the usual order of things. Cicero is unmoved:

> Indeed, it is a strange-disposed time;
> But men may construe things after their fashion,
> Clean from the purpose of the things themselves.   (33–35)

Cicero's membership in the conspiracy is proposed by Cassius but rejected by Brutus (II.i.139–152). Cicero is not at the Capitol during Caesar's assassination and is mentioned only once more, in accord with historical fact. Brutus and Messala have fled to Sardis and are discussing events back in Rome. The triumvirate, it seems, processing their enemy list, have trumped up charges against and then executed between seventy and a hundred senators, "Cicero being one" (IV.iii.178).

In his use of Cicero as a minor character, Shakespeare demonstrates his skill in addressing several audiences simultaneously. Those playgoers to whom Cicero's name did not ring any particular bell were not distracted by references to him; such references are brief and do not impede the plot. Those who remembered Cicero as a major part of their education would have welcomed him here as a kind of authentication that they were indeed in ancient Rome. Anne Barton has suggested that Shakespeare, by "keeping the enormous memory of Cicero alive in his tragedy," reminds his audience that Rome was "the city of orators and rhetoricians," where "the art of persuasion was cultivated, for better or for worse, to an extent unparalleled in any other society."[13] As we will focus on questions of rhetoric at a later point in this chapter, the spirit of Cicero might well remain in our minds as well.

Lepidus and Octavius

Highest ranking of the newcomers in the last two acts are Antony's fellow triumvirates, Lepidus and Octavius. Lepidus appears only once, to be sent immediately away and disparaged by Antony as unworthy of respect and "meet to be sent on errands" (IV.i.13). Octavius then defends Lepidus as a "tried and valiant soldier." In *Antony and Cleopatra* it will be Antony, in a more generous mood, who treats Lepidus well and Octavius who accuses him of treason and imprisons him. The historical Lepidus survived these misfortunes and eventually died a natural death, though he never regained any real power.

Octavius, who appears in only three scenes (IV.i, V.i, and V.v), is a minor character but a memorable one. Many of Shakespeare's playgoers would have known that he later became Augustus Caesar, the first emperor and originator of the "Roman Peace," or "Pax Romana," the state of comparative calm that obtained in the Mediterranean world for the next two hundred years. He is also the Caesar Augustus of the Christmas story; he will send out "a decree . . . that all the world should be taxed."[14] Audience members who do not recall these associations nevertheless find Octavius an impressive if rather frightening figure—calm, self-sufficient, in control. Unlike many of the other characters, Octavius feels no need to be part of a group and does not care whether people like him.

Octavius's young age makes this imperturbability the more striking. Shakespeare here follows Plutarch and history; Octavius was in his nineteenth year at the death of Julius Caesar, his great-uncle, who had adopted him as his heir. Octavius's youth works to his advantage because it allows both his enemies and his allies to underestimate him. Cassius, for example, taunts him as a "peevish schoolboy" (V.i.61) before the battle of Philippi.

Antony, too, misjudges Octavius when at Philippi he tries to give him an order, telling him to lead his army forward on the left side of the field. Octavius replies that he will take the right side. When Antony expostulates, Octavius calmly replies, "I do not cross you; but I will do so" (V.i.20). The subject, it would appear, is closed. A few lines later, for the first time in the play, Antony addresses Octavius as "Caesar."

Friends of Brutus in Acts IV and V

Also new to the play's later scenes are a swarm of minor characters taken from Plutarch. These figures are more confusing to readers of the printed text than to the audience at a stage or film production. The reader, seeing definite names and speech prefixes, is aware of their sudden appearance and his lack of familiarity with them. On stage or screen, the newcomers function simply as voices from a crowd, men in armor carrying spears, and since the action involves military camps and battles, the audience tends to accept these anonymous figures as a natural part of the setting.

Some of these men appear to be trusted friends of the main characters. Lucilius, for example, carries confidential messages between Brutus and Antony (IV.ii) and later, on the battlefield, pretends to be Brutus (V.iv.12). Titinius attends the policy meeting in Brutus's tent at Sardis (IV.iii.140), though he does not contribute to the discussion and becomes the inadvertent cause of Cassius's suicide; Cassius despairs when he wrongly thinks Titinius has been captured. Titinius commits suicide when he finds Cassius's body (V.iii.90).

Messala, an experienced and high-ranking officer, serves as a confidant to Brutus and Cassius at various points (IV.iii and V.1). Messala is later captured by Octavius and taken into his service (V.v.60), along with several of Brutus's other supporters.

A number of minor characters in Acts IV and V are imported from Plutarch to perform only one function, after which they vanish. (Stage and film productions often combine these rather miscellaneous roles and thus end up with a conveniently smaller number of characters.) The entire job of Varrus and Claudio (as spelled in the First Folio), for example, is to sleep in Brutus's tent and fail to see the ghost of Caesar (IV.iii.245). Dardanius, Clito, and Volumnius step from Plutarch into the play solely to refuse Brutus's request that they help him kill himself (V.v.1–51); their companion Strato, also unheard of previously in the play, takes on the assignment. Similarly, Pindarus, a Parthian slave belonging to Cassius, assists his master's suicide (iii.46).

Another unexpected minor character, "young Cato," proclaims his name about the battlefield—"I am the son of Marcus Cato, ho!" (V.iv.4)—and is promptly killed. The historical dimension, which some of Shakespeare's audience would have known, adds resonance to this otherwise abrupt and perplexing incident from Plutarch. Marcus Cato of Utica, the young man's father, was an opponent of Julius Caesar, "a foe to tyrants," as his son has just stated. Portia, Brutus's late wife, was Cato's daughter and reminded her husband of the fact when she asserted her right to his confidence (II.i.295). The senior Cato had killed himself after Julius Caesar defeated him in battle; Brutus alludes to this event in conversation with Cassius (V.i.101).

As unexpected as young Cato but lacking a family connection is the "camp poet" who interrupts the quarrel between Brutus and Cassius (IV. iii.124–138). The incident is taken from Plutarch.

Finally, Brutus's young servant Lucius reappears in Act IV, having accompanied his master from Rome to Sardis. As we have seen him do earlier, he fetches and carries, in the middle of the night when necessary, and here he also displays a musical talent, providing Brutus with a "sleepy tune" (iii.267). In doing so he puts himself to sleep and, thus, like the two guards, misses seeing Caesar's ghost.

Lucius is an alert, intelligent boy. He notices a letter in Brutus's study that "did not lie there when I went to bed" (II.i.38), and on the morning of the assassination Portia tells him to go to the Capitol and "take good note / What Caesar doth, what suitors press to him" (II.iv.14–15.) He enhances Brutus's characterization by bringing out a generous side of his master's nature: "Gentle knave, good night; / I will not do thee so much wrong to wake thee" (IV.iii.269–270).

Lucius is similar to Calphurnia, Portia, and the aged senator Publius in that he represents an innocent person touched by events over which he has no control. Shakespeare does not indicate what becomes of Lucius at the end of the play, and since he is not a historical character, we cannot look him up and find out. Lucius's fate, like so much of *Julius Caesar*, is ambiguous.

LANGUAGE: USE OF PROSE AND VERSE

One sometimes encounters the suspiciously simple statement that Shakespeare's upper-class characters speak verse (that is to say, blank verse, unrhymed iambic pentameter), while his lower-class characters speak prose. This observation is true by and large, but it does not hold in every case. *Julius Caesar* offers some interesting exceptions.

In two instances the general rule appears justified. The cobbler in the play's opening scene (I.i.1–31) speaks prose, while the two tribunes speak verse. Again, the Roman mob speaks prose when it seizes Cinna the Poet, while Cinna first tries to defend himself in blank verse but shifts into prose, perhaps in a futile effort to gain the sympathy of his attackers by echoing their mode of speech (III.iii.1–39).

Casca, however, hardly a lower-class character—he is a senator and a former schoolmate of Cassius—addresses Brutus and Cassius in prose, telling them "in his sour fashion" about Caesar's being offered and then refusing the crown (I.ii.235–288). Presumably Shakespeare used prose here to express the brusque personality Casca has here assumed.

Equally brusque, and with overtones of desperate urgency, is the letter written to Caesar by Artemidorus, who is a literate person and clearly a well-informed one. The letter stands out from the blank verse that surrounds it (II.iii.1–10), so that its different sound patterns catch the audience's attention. When he has finished reading the letter, Artemidorus shifts into iambic pentameter.

The most frequently noticed of *Julius Caesar*'s prose passages is Brutus's speech in the Forum (III.ii.12–47). Since Brutus's social status is hardly open to question, we can assume that Shakespeare wrote the passage in prose in order to portray Brutus's self-image of plainspoken efficiency. Brutus's speech also contrasts metrically with Antony's, where we find a full use of the resonance, depth, and color of the blank verse in which most of the play is written.

Julius Caesar's blank verse is flexible but strong, adapting itself to the play's variegated moods and circumstances. In the English language, unrhymed iambic pentameter has the feel of spontaneous speech because so many metrical effects can be attained with it. Yet its underlying rhythm binds the sounds into a coherent pattern and enhances the integrity of the whole message.[15]

A completely regular blank verse line would contain ten syllables, alternating stressed with unstressed syllables and beginning with an unstressed one: ti-*tum*, ti-*tum*, ti-*tum*, ti-*tum*, ti-*tum*. Such regularity, repeated line after line, would become excruciatingly monotonous quickly.[16] Consequently the subtleties of the rhythm vary from line to line, and the same line is often capable of different renditions. Punctuation and the sense of the words also allow a great deal of variety in the placement of long or short pauses. For example, these lines are built on the basic iambic pentameter pattern:

> The fault, dear Brutus, lies not in our stars,
> But in ourselves, that we are underlings.   (I.ii.140–141)

One senses the five strong beats coming through very insistently. And yet, as a few experiments will show, some of the syllables can be variously stressed. The first two strong beats are fairly content to remain where the basic pattern puts them: "The *fault*, dear *Brut*us." But the rest of the line gets wriggly. "*Lies* not *in* our *stars*"? Or, "Lies *not* in our *stars*"? Either can be effective, or one could work out other patterns as well

Again, in the same example, the pauses within the lines have a built-in variation that keeps them from sounding too much alike. The punctuation gives a clue. In the first line, one would pause after "fault," again after "Brutus," and again at the end of the line; in the second line, one would pause after "ourselves." However, an actor trying to show the urgent tone of Cassius's argument might omit the pause at the end of the first line, running the phrases together, "Not in our stars but in ourselves." The pause after "ourselves" would be retained in order to let the preceding words sink in, but the actor might then add another pause: "That we are [pause] underlings." The final syllable might be given a more than usually strong stress, emphasizing Cassius's scorn.

Often a change of stress is built into a line, particularly the "reversed foot" variation in which the opening syllable is strong rather than, as in the more usual pattern, weak. Such a line is usually followed by a return to regular iambics:

> Cowards die many times before their deaths,
> The valiant never taste of death but once.   (II.ii.32–33)

Occasionally the basic pattern gives a hop and a skip. Brutus, preparing to relax with a book after a hard day, relaxes his meter as well:

> Let me see, let me see; is not the leaf turn'd down
> Where I left reading? Here it is, I think.   (IV.iii.273–274)

Always, however, and no matter how far-fetched the metrical variation may be, the underlying rhythmic pattern may be felt, holding the play together. For example, if a passage ends in the midst of a five-beat line, the next speaker quite often picks up the rhythm and completes the line. Here Calphurnia has been describing the supernatural apparitions of the night:

> O Caesar, these things are beyond all use,
> And I do fear them.

Caesar responds:

> What can be avoided,
> Whose end is purpos'd by the mighty gods?   (II.ii.25–27)

In some of his earlier plays—for example, *A Midsummer Night's Dream* and *Romeo and Juliet*—Shakespeare often varies the blank verse with a rhyming couplet or even a rhyming passage. Rhyme is not used often in *Julius Caesar*, but it does appear occasionally. Often the effect is to end a scene on some special note—triumphant, ominous, wistful—or to mark a transition, pointing ahead to the future. Cassius, for example, gloats about the progress of his scheme:

> And after this, let Caesar seat him sure,
> For we will shake him, or worse days endure.   (I.ii.316–317)

Similarly, Artemidorus, having read aloud his prose letter, takes on an oracular tone, aided by the Elizabethan pronunciation of vowels, which are now sounded differently:

> If thou read this, O Caesar, thou may'st live;
> If not, the fates with traitors do contrive.   (II.iii.13–14)

Brutus marks a chronological transition when he opens the second phase (as Shakespeare presents it) of the battle of Philippi:

> 'Tis three a clock; and, Romans, yet ere night
> We shall try fortune in a second fight.   (V.iii.109–110)

Again, rhyme gives Brutus's words a knell-like ring when he undertakes his suicide:

> Caesar, now be still,
> I kill'd not thee with half so good a will.   (V.v.50–51)

A rhyming couplet concludes the play and enhances both Octavius's victory and the audience's feeling of having witnessed a complete action:

> So call the field to rest, and let's away
> To part the glories of this happy day.   (V.v.80–81)

LANGUAGE AS RHETORIC: BRUTUS AND ANTONY IN THE FORUM

Julius Caesar is a play woven of rhetoric. Characters continually endeavor to persuade someone to do something, successfully or unsuccessfully as the case may be. Cassius persuades Brutus to join his cause, Portia persuades Brutus to tell her what is troubling him, Calphurnia fails to persuade Caesar to stay at home. Even when the characters are alone, they engage in persuasion. As Brutus ponders the consequences of killing Caesar, he is busily persuading himself to accept a conclusion he has already reached, and he begins by stating this conclusion: "It must be by his death" (II.i.10).

It is typical of this play that one of its crucial battles should take the form of a rhetorical contest. Which speaker can win the approval of the Roman mob: Brutus or Antony? Each constructs his argument carefully and brings to bear the devices he thinks will be most effective. Shakespeare here shows his familiarity with the techniques of rhetoric as taught in the schools that he and many members of his audience had attended.

According to these teachings, derived from classical Latin models, the basic strategies of persuasion are *logos*, or convincing the listeners' minds through reason and logic; *pathos*, or rousing the listeners' emotions to anger, pity, or other incentives to action; and *ethos*, or presenting oneself as a reliable person possessed of goodwill toward the listeners, and therefore to be trusted.[17] Both Brutus and Antony use these strategies, but with differing degrees of emphasis. Each differs as well in his sentence structure, his choice of images, and the extent to which he interacts with the crowd.

Brutus Takes the First Turn

Brutus, unfortunately for him, does not realize that he is part of a contest. He assumes that he is in control, that Antony is as subservient as he has just professed to be, and that Antony's speech will consist merely of a few respectful words about Caesar. "You shall not in your funeral speech blame us," Brutus has told Antony (III.i.245), and Antony has humbly agreed.

Perhaps because he thinks himself so thoroughly in the right that he expects no opposition, Brutus gives a brief address of fewer than four hundred words, explaining his reasons for killing Caesar and giving the crowd an opportunity to agree with him. His sentences, though in prose, are extremely rhythmic, almost hypnotic, and are built of parallel elements:

> Had you rather Caesar were living, and die all slaves, than that Caesar were dead, to live all freemen? As Caesar lov'd me, I weep for him; as he was fortunate, I rejoice at it; as he was valiant, I honor him; but, as he was ambitious, I slew him. There is tears for his love; joy for his fortune; honor for his valor; and death for his ambition.   (III.ii.22–29)

The major appeal here is to *logos*. Various attributes in Caesar call for various responses, Brutus implies, and he, Brutus, has quite properly come up with them all. What the listeners fail to notice, being swept away by the inevitable progression of the grammatical structure and taking for granted that the ideas expressed are similarly inevitable, is that Brutus has not given any proof for his claim. Ambition in a ruler may be a bad thing, but not necessarily; Caesar had not yet turned into a tyrant and might never do so. He had not actually enslaved any free Romans. Brutus's stance is based on a hypothetical view of the future. It is a future in which he sincerely believes, having earlier talked himself into it when he compared the present innocent Caesar to a serpent's egg (II.i.32), and this sincerity adds weight to his appeal. Obviously, in his own opinion, he has done the reasonable, the only sensible thing.

Logic, or the appearance of logic, also strengthens the process by which Brutus proves to the crowd that nobody could possibly object to his action:

> Who is here so base that would be a bondman? If any, speak, for him have I offended. Who is here so rude that would not be a Roman? If any, speak, for him have I offended. Who is here so vile that would not love his country? If any, speak, for him have I offended. I pause for a reply.   (29–34)

Not surprisingly, nobody in the crowd volunteers to join any of these categories, and Brutus stands exonerated: "Then none have I offended."

Besides *logos*, Brutus emphasizes *ethos* in presenting himself as a reliable and trustworthy person. He has begun on this note:

> Romans, countrymen, and lovers, hear me for my cause, and be silent, that you may hear. Believe me for mine honor, and have respect to mine honor, that you may believe.   (13–16)

At the end of his speech, Brutus returns to his vision of himself as an honorable and impartial person: "As I slew my best lover for the good of Rome, I have the same dagger for myself, when it shall please my country to need my death" (44–47). The crowd, enthusiastically on his side, shouts, "Live, Brutus, live!"

Brutus has also paid attention to *pathos*. His addressing his countrymen as "lovers" implies a certain emotion on both sides. The love that he professes for Rome—"Not that I lov'd Caesar less, but that I lov'd Rome more"—becomes an argument in his favor; patriotism made him do it. Brutus arouses his listeners' passions as well, so that they support his cause.

On its own terms, Brutus's speech is a successful one. The audience can assume that it would have solidified the conspirators' position were it not for Antony, who had other plans and was able to execute them.

Antony Makes His Move

Antony enters with the corpse of Caesar, a most effective visual aid and the strongest card he holds, although he does not play it immediately. (In some productions, Antony carries the corpse in his arms; in others it is brought in by attendants. Either way, at this point the corpse is covered by Caesar's mantle.)

Like Brutus, Antony appeals to *logos*, *pathos*, and *ethos*, in varying proportions. His sentences are not as tightly knit as Brutus's, relying less on parallel structure. His ideas flow more loosely, turning in unexpected directions or even halting altogether:

> Bear with me,
> My heart is in the coffin there with Caesar,
> And I must pause till it come back to me.   (105–107)

Antony uses a great deal more imagery, figurative language, than Brutus has done. The above quotation, in which Antony's heart wanders about on its own, illustrates this figurative richness, along with Antony's famous opening line: "Friends, Romans, countrymen, lend me your ears." These apparently detachable body parts would in rhetorical terminology demonstrate the use of *synecdoche*, or the substitution of a part for the whole.[18] The heart and the ears represent, respectively, their owners' whole selves—in particular their attention and ability to concentrate.

Blank verse is the ideal medium for the kind of persuasion Antony has undertaken. Its combination of variety and cohesiveness is perfectly suited to imagaic richness, subtle argument, and oratorical flourish.

As a recurrent strategy, Antony employs *paralipsis*, the assertion that he is not going to reveal the information he is in fact revealing, or, more broadly, that he is not doing what he is in fact doing. He begins with just such a disclaimer—"I come to bury Caesar, not to praise him"—and then goes on, of course, to supply evidence that adds up to praise of Caesar:

> He hath brought many captives home to Rome
> Whose ransoms did the general coffers fill;
> Did this in Caesar seem ambitious?   (88–90)

"Friends, Romans, Countrymen." Antony (Owen Teale) gets the crowd's attention at Stratford-upon-Avon, 1991. Reproduced by courtesy of the Shakespeare Centre Library, Stratford-upon-Avon.

Antony is directly attacking Brutus's use of *logos* in these lines. If Brutus killed Caesar because Caesar was ambitious, but Caesar in fact was not ambitious, then Brutus's reasoning is clearly based on a faulty premise. The crowd begins to agree, being especially impressed with Caesar's rejection of a kingly crown at the Lupercalian celebration:

> Mark'd ye his words? He would not take the crown,
> Therefore 'tis certain he was not ambitious. (112–113)

The logic here is far from watertight, since Caesar might have refused the crown out of pretended modesty while waiting for a later offer, but Antony's listeners prefer a quick conclusion.

Another continuing device, woven through the speech, is Antony's ironic repetition of the phrase "honorable men." The conspirators in general, and Brutus in particular, are, he asserts, "honorable." At first the word sounds innocuous, and the crowd takes it at face value. They are at this early point decidedly pro-Brutus and have only reluctantly agreed to listen to Antony, murmuring, "'Twere best he speak no harm of Brutus here" (68). But as Antony's references to honorable men continue—nine of them in all—the discrepancy between the word and its context builds into ferocious sarcasm. By the seventh repetition, the tide has turned. The crowd is shouting for Antony to read Caesar's will, and Antony demurs:

> I have o'ershot myself to tell you of it.
> I fear I wrong the honorable men
> Whose daggers have stabb'd Caesar. (150–152)

In their response, the crowd repeats the phrase on their own, now fully aware of the irony: "They were traitors; honorable men!"

In his use of *ethos*, or the creation of rapport with his listeners, Antony is masterful. Brutus has permitted a certain amount of interaction, asking for the crowd's approval of the killing, but this response was brief, and Brutus remained obviously in control. Antony, on the other hand, pretends to be controlled by the crowd, even to his physical movements. Before he reads Caesar's will, he explains, he wants to show the crowd "the corpse of Caesar . . . him that made the will" (158–159). But to do so he will need to leave the pulpit where he has been standing. "Shall I descend? And will you give me leave?" The crowd kindly permits this change of elevation: "You shall have leave."

Antony also creates *ethos* by portraying himself as a reliable person, worthy of trust because he is not up to any oratorical tricks and is motivated purely by loyalty:

> I am no orator, as Brutus is,
> But (as you know me all) a plain blunt man
> That love my friend. (217–219)

In claiming to be no orator, Antony supplies a dazzling example of his characteristic use of *paralipsis*.

In *pathos*, or the display of his own emotions and the rousing of emotion in his
listeners, Antony is far ahead of Brutus. He may have an advantage in that Brutus,
as an adherent of the Stoic philosophy, is in the habit of downplaying his emotions.
Antony seems to revel in them. When he shows the crowd Caesar's body, he begins
with the garment Caesar was wearing when he was killed, and he draws the crowd
into a personal connection with it: "You all do know this mantle" (170). Caesar
made frequent public appearances, and it is possible that some members of the
crowd do remember this mantle; but even if they do not, Antony's manner, intimate and confidential, turning his listeners into a united family with memories in
common, would make them think they do.

Antony proceeds to display the bloodied holes in the mantle, one by one:

> Look, in this place ran Cassius's dagger through;
> See what a rent the envious Casca made.   (174–175)

These details are created for rhetorical effect, since Antony was not present when
Caesar was killed and would hardly have remembered who had made which hole if
he had been. The effect is what matters. Antony continues to highlight Caesar's
blood in an imaginative simile. Brutus has just done his part:

> And as he pluck'd his cursed steel away,
> Mark how the blood of Caesar followed it,
> As rushing out of doors to be resolv'd
> If Brutus so unkindly knock'd, or no.   (178–181)

The ironic contrast between a murderer with a knife and a guest at the door calls
attention to Brutus's abuse of Caesar's friendship and hospitality, recently demonstrated, as the audience remembers, when Brutus called at Caesar's house only that
morning.

Antony then plays on the meaning of the word "fall," expanding it from a literal
to a metaphorical connotation, and personifies the abstract noun "treason" by let-
ting it wave a banner or perform a musical fanfare:

> O, what a fall was there, my countrymen!
> Then I, and you, and all of us fell down,
> Whil'st bloody treason flourish'd over us.   (190–192)

Throughout his speech, Antony gives directions to his hearers, pointing their energy into specified channels. The crowd is to become inflamed, shed tears, and finally rise in mutiny. This they do. As they rush away in search of fire, Antony
retains his rhetorical mode for his own personal benefit and indulges in a parting
personification:

Now let it work. Mischief, thou art afoot,
Take thou what course thou wilt.   (260–261)

He has won the contest, as he well knows. Confirming news soon arrives of his opponents' flight: "Brutus and Cassius / Are rid like madmen through the gates of Rome" (268–269).

NOTES

1. Freytag's *Technik des Dramas* appeared in 1863. A translation of the second edition of 1896, *Technique of the Drama: An Exposition of Dramatic Composition and Art*, by Elias J. MacEwan, has been reprinted (St. Clair Shores, Mich.: Scholarly Press, 1969). See pp. 114–140.

2. Harley Granville-Barker feels this moment is the more dramatic for its low-key effect; it is "significant in its insignificance." *Prefaces to Shakespeare: Julius Caesar* (Portsmouth, N.H.: Heineman, 1995 [1925]), p. 50. For this identification of the play's turning point, Granville-Barker acknowledges R. G. Moulton, *Shakespeare as a Dramatic Artist* (Oxford: Oxford University Press, 1906), pp. 197–198.

3. *Aristotle's Poetics: A Translation and Commentary for Students of Literature*, trans. Leon Golden, commentary by O. B. Hardison, Jr. (Englewood Cliffs, N.J.: Prentice-Hall, 1968), p. 11.

4. Considerable critical attention has been given to this question of ambiguity. See, for example, Ernest Schanzer, "*Julius Caesar* as a Problem Play," in Leonard F. Dean, ed., *Twentieth Century Interpretations of Julius Caesar* (Englewood Cliffs, N.J.: Prentice-Hall, 1968), pp. 67–72.

5. Leah Scragg, *Discovering Shakespeare's Meaning: An Introduction to the Study of Shakespeare's Dramatic Structures* (London: Longman, 1988, 1994), p. 152.

6. Alexander Leggatt, *Shakespeare's Political Drama: The History Plays and the Roman Plays* (London: Routledge, 1988), p. 153.

7. David Bevington, Introduction to *Julius Caesar* (New York: Bantam Classics, 1988), pp. xx–xxi.

8. Geoffrey Miles, *Shakespeare and the Constant Romans* (Oxford: Clarendon Press, 1996), p. 139.

9. Granville-Barker, *Prefaces*, p. 104.

10. E.A.J. Honigman, *Shakespeare: Seven Tragedies: The Dramatist's Manipulation of Response* (New York: Harper & Row, 1976), p. 38.

11. T.J.B. Spencer, ed., *Shakespeare's Plutarch* (Harmondsworth: Penguin, 1964), p. 163.

12. Charles Boyce, "Casca," in *Shakespeare A to Z* (New York: Roundtable Press, 1990), p. 95.

13. Anne Barton, "Rhetoric in Ancient Rome," in Harold Bloom, ed., *William Shakespeare's Julius Caesar* (New York: Chelsea House, 1988), p. 80.

14. Luke 2:1, quoted from the King James Bible of 1607. In the Geneva Bible, available to Shakespeare's 1599 audience, Augustus Caesar sends out a "commandment."

15. Northrop Frye discusses the flexible qualities of poetic rhythm, pointing out that "iambic pentameter provides a field of syncopation in which stress and meter can to some

extent neutralize one another." See his *Anatomy of Criticism: Four Essays* (Princeton, N.J.: Princeton University Press, 1957), pp. 251–262.

16. A technical analysis of metrical patterns in *Julius Caesar* may be found in Appendix A, "Outline of Shakespeare's Prosody," in Arthur D. Innes, ed., *Julius Caesar* (Boston: D. C. Heath, 1907), pp. 127–133. Innes devotes special attention to "Lines of Doubtful Scansion," p. 133.

17. Sister Miriam Joseph, in *Shakespeare's Use of the Arts of Language* (New York: Hafner, 1947, 1966), examines these concepts in detail. In her discussion of Antony's speech, pp. 283–286, Sister Miriam Joseph puts special stress on the reaction of the crowd and compares Antony's rhetorical devices with those used by Iago in *Othello*.

18. Numerous handbooks to rhetorical terms can be of assistance here. Richard A. Lanham's *Handlist of Rhetorical Terms: A Guide for Students of English Literature* (Berkeley and Los Angeles: University of California Press, 1968), is particularly inclusive and well arranged.

4

THEMES

A theme, as students generally have little difficulty in grasping, is different from a plot summary or a character description, either of which is concerned with the finite particulars of the literary work under consideration. Themes deal with universals that form a bridge between the lives of the fictional characters in the literary work and the life of the reader (or, in a dramatic work, of the audience member).

In experiencing *Julius Caesar*, we are aware that we do not live in ancient Rome or fight battles with sword and shield, that these people and these times are remote from us; and, of course, we are also aware that although Shakespeare based his play on historical records, he has produced a work of creative art that inhabits its own world, so to speak, its own dimension. Just the same, because of the universal themes that we recognize, consciously or unconsciously, as analogous to our own lives, this faraway world becomes accessible and significant to us.

Themes are often supported by patterns of imagery, and in drama the term "image" can be taken beyond the mere limited denotations of metaphor, personification, and other rhetorical devices. A play is by nature a metaphor, a representation; the audience knows that the figures on the stage are actors, that when the performance is over they will go on with their individual lives. Consequently, even quite literal ingredients of a play can function as images, whether or not verbal description is involved. If an actor takes out a dagger onstage, the dagger is (within the metaphorical world of the play) a real one, not a verbal comparison; yet it can take part in a pattern of imagery, some of which is rhetorical and some of which is tangibly in view, and thus point to one or more of the play's themes.

Themes often overlap, or link up with one another. In *Julius Caesar*, for example, the same image (Calphurnia's dream, say, of Caesar's statue spouting blood) might support a theme of violence and destruction if viewed from one angle, or of omens and prophecies if viewed from another. Often, too, we can perceive a large-scale, overarching theme encompassing a number of other themes—subthemes so to speak. In *Julius Caesar*, the major theme of order versus disorder encompasses many of the more specific themes we will examine: time, both linear and cyclical; the cosmos with its circling spheres; fire and blood; religion, dreams, and portents; and the theme of man himself, his particular identity, especially in relation to the animal kingdom.

TIME: CYCLICAL AND LINEAR

As a play concerned with a pivotal moment in history, *Julius Caesar* is connected ex officio, so to speak, with a thematic pattern of time. This pattern can be seen as a combination of cyclical time, in which seasons recur and events reecho, and of linear time, which advances inexorably into the future and allows no going back. As Northrop Frye observes with regard to linear time:

> The basis of the tragic vision is being in time, the sense of the one-directional quality of life, where everything happens once and for all, where every act brings unavoidable and fateful consequences, and where all experience vanishes, not simply into the past, but into nothingness, annihilation. . . . The mood of tragedy preserves our ambiguous and paradoxical feeling about death; it is inevitable and always happens, and yet, when it does happen, it carries with it some sense of the unnatural and premature. The naiveté of Marlowe's Tamburlaine, astonished by the fact that *he* should die when he has been wading through other men's blood for years, is an example, and even Shakespeare's Caesar, so thoroughly disciplined in his view of death in general, still finds his actual death a surprise.[1]

Despite the unstoppable and unrevisable march of linear time, forever advancing into the unknown, cyclical time also plays a large part in human awareness.[2] Cyclical time is reassuring because we feel that an orderly progression is being followed. Sunrise is succeeded by sunset; the seasons follow one another; holidays are observed according to an agreed-upon schedule. We then go a bit further and assume we can predict what is going to happen, establish the cycles to be followed, and, in short, project our own ideas upon the future.

Cassius Tries to Control Time

These assumptions of power may appear to come true, in life and in literature, but in *Julius Caesar* the conspirators' attempts to combine linear and cyclical time and to dictate the future brings them to ironic grief. Caesar lies dead, fallen at the foot of Pompey's statue; his killers stoop and bathe their hands in his blood. They have, they think, succeeded. They will be welcomed by the people and hailed as liberators. Cassius then envisions the present moment as a recurring cyclical event in this favorable future:

> Stoop, then, and wash. How many ages hence
> Shall this our lofty scene be acted over
> In states unborn and accents yet unknown!   (III.i.111–113)

Brutus, pleased with this vision, chimes in. The murder they have just done, the irrevocable violence of the unique moment, is now calmly wrapped in theatrical ritual, a scene destined to come around again:

> How many times shall Caesar bleed in sport,
> That now on Pompey's basis lies along,
> No worthier than the dust! (114–116)

And Cassius takes care to give himself and his colleagues their proper glory in these future reenactments:

> So oft as that shall be,
> So often shall the knot of us be call'd
> The men that gave their country liberty. (116–118)

To the audience, the irony inherent in this passage is overwhelming. We are watching this scene, as Cassius said, being "acted over." The actors speak English, a language that developed many centuries after the events they are portraying and that would have been to the Romans "accents yet unknown." Shakespeare's sovereign state, England, was unborn as a political entity when Caesar was assassinated, even though this distant northern island was part of the Roman world. Finally, the actor lying on the stage is bleeding, one assumes, barring some accident of mortality, only in sport.

A further time-related irony surrounds the Ides of March. Before Caesar's assassination, this date was simply part of the Roman calendar, indicating the middle of the month. (It would fall ordinarily on the thirteenth or the fifteenth.) Cassius and Brutus in their moment of triumph might well have assumed that future Ides of March would include a celebration of their deed, thus giving the date a special and joyous content. Instead, events so fall out that Brutus next mentions the date in the midst of a bitter quarrel, when upbraiding Cassius for supporting a colleague who dishonorably took bribes:

> Remember March, the Ides of March remember:
> Did not great Julius bleed for justice' sake? (IV.iii.18–19)

Today the phrase "Ides of March" is indeed associated with the death of Caesar, but it is remembered as the Soothsayer phrased it and has come to mean any presage of coming disaster: "Beware the Ides of March!" (I.ii.18).

Cassius's dream of being ritually honored in the theaters of the future comes to nothing. Instead, he ends up taking an ironic comfort in cyclical patterns at the battle of Philippi. The revolving calendar has arrived at his own birthday. This present day, as Cassius experiences it, is, of course, unique in linear time, but because of time's coexisting cyclical nature, it is also associated with his other birthdays, and especially with the first one:

> This day I breathed first. Time is come round.
> And where I did begin, there shall I end.
> My life is run his compass.   (V.iii.23–25)

The combination of cyclical and linear time that Cassius here invokes might be imagined as a circular stairway. As he ascends to a certain point, he finds himself directly above the same point on the circles below him—his birthday, as it happens. Yet the stair on which he is standing is distinct unto itself; it is not identical with the earlier ones, and he cannot turn around and go back to them.

In his lamentation over Cassius's body, Titinius uses images associated with cyclical time, sunset, and changing seasons:

> O setting sun!
> As in thy red rays thou dost sink tonight,
> So in his red blood Cassius's day is set!
> The sun of Rome is set. Our day is gone,
> Clouds, dews, and dangers come; our deeds are done.   (V.iii.60–64)

The Striking Clock and the Theme of Time

An anachronism that occasionally puzzles readers, and can be related to both linear and cyclical time, is the clock that interrupts the conspirators' meeting (II.i.191). (Clocks as we know them, with wheels, escapements, weights, and striking mechanisms, were invented in the fourteenth century.) Sigurd Burckhardt has argued that this seeming anachronism was deliberate on Shakespeare's part and points to a thematic connection with history and politics.[3]

The so-called orchard scene (II.i) contains numerous references to time, as Burckhardt points out. Brutus, alone with his thoughts, depicts himself as unsure of the time of day, or rather, of night:

> I cannot by the progress of the stars
> Give guess how near to day.   (2–3)

Shortly afterward, he asks Lucius to inform him of the time of month, and here Burckhardt assumes that the First Folio's reading represents Shakespeare's intention and that the emendation (to "Ides of March") usually made by present-day editors is misleading. In the First Folio, Brutus says, "Is not tomorrow, boy, the first of March?" (40). Then, as Burckhardt points out, "his servant boy has to inform him that he is off by a full fourteen days."[4]

More time references follow. In Burckhardt's words, "While Brutus and Cassius withdraw . . . to the background and confer in inaudible whispers, the secondary conspirators take the center of the stage and engage in a seemingly pointless dispute over the points of the compass, the point of the sun's rising, and the time of year."

After Brutus and Cassius return to the discussion and the assassination plans are made, the clock strikes three times. (Incidentally, it will be at three o'clock, though in the afternoon rather than at night, when according to Shakespeare Brutus decides to renew the battle of Philippi in V.iii.109.)

Shakespeare's purpose in making so concentrated a group of time references, Burckhardt suggests, is to remind his audience, who in 1599 would have been alert to this matter, of the significance of the calendar in politics: "Caesar's fame rested in good part on his institution of the Julian calendar. Plutarch—Shakespeare's source—praises this great reform and mentions it as one of the reasons why Caesar was hated; the Roman conservatives felt it to be an arbitrary and tyrannical interference with the course of nature."

A second item of calendar politics had occurred in Shakespeare's world, only seventeen years previously. In 1582, Pope Gregory had reformed the Julian calendar, which during the intervening centuries had drifted ten days or so out of synchronization with the sun and the constellations, and this seemingly useful project had become a bone of bitter contention between Catholic and Protestant countries. Protestant states refused to adopt the new calendar because it had been created by a Catholic authority. "Thus," says Burckhardt, "a situation existed in Europe exactly analogous to that of Rome in 44 B.C. It was a time of confusion and uncertainty, when the most basic category by which men order their experience seemed to have become unstable and untrustworthy, subject to arbitrary political manipulation."

By trying to return Rome to the days of the old Roman Republic, Burckhardt claims, Brutus himself has become an anachronism, unaware of the time, just as he has shown himself to be in a more literal sense. The Roman mob is unable to understand what he was trying to do. In acclaiming Brutus, they cried, "Let him be Caesar!" (III.ii.51). "Nothing shows so clearly as this shout of applause how totally the audience has missed Brutus's point and how totally Brutus has misjudged his audience."[5]

THE COSMOS AND HUMAN SOCIETY

The concept of order, always of significance in Shakespeare's work, informs the theme of the heavenly cosmos. Ordinarily the universe is expected to display a pattern of harmony. The stars revolve in their courses, and astronomers confidently predict what next will happen overhead. Within this orderliness, however, we find some disorder. Some stars do not seem to have courses. Comets are among these, and here present-day stargazers have an advantage; thanks to long-term observations and complex calculations, we know that comets do have orbits, albeit oddly shaped ones, and do recur at predictable intervals.[6] Calphurnia associates comets with grievous disorder as she tries to convince Caesar that the heavenly commotion of the previous night refers to him personally:

> When beggars die there are no comets seen;
> The heavens themselves blaze forth the deaths of princes.   (II.ii.30–31)

Caesar, however, as if to oppose Calphurnia's suggestion, later compares himself to the most stable of heavenly bodies: "I am as constant as the northern star" (III.i.60).

Aside from comets (and eclipses, though these do not come into *Julius Caesar*), the serenely harmonious cosmos might sometimes harbor disorder in the "sublunar" sphere, the realm below the moon, which surrounded the earth and its imperfections.[7] Here storms could take place, and one does, with accompanying thunder, lightning, and fiery portents. Casca, terrified, invokes a macrocosm-microcosm pattern; events in the celestial world are to be seen as parallel with human society:

> Who ever knew the heavens menace so? . . .
> It is the part of man to fear and tremble
> When the most mighty gods by tokens send
> Such mighty heralds to astonish us.   (I.iii.44, 54–56)

Cassius agrees with Casca's implication—that the heavens are aligned with man's domain and specifically with Rome—and suggests a reason. The disordered heavens reflect a disordered and imbalanced society:

> Now could I, Casca, name to thee a man
> Most like this dreadful night . . .
> A man no mightier than thyself, or me,
> In personal action, yet prodigious grown,
> And fearful, as these strange eruptions are.   (72–73, 76–78)

The agent of this imbalance, perturbation, and unnatural disproportion, as Casca then correctly guesses, is, according to Cassius, Caesar.

Rome, the seat of human society in this play, thus reflects two aspects of the cosmos: the unchanging constancy so sought after by Caesar and the unstable turbulence initiated by the conspirators and then used against them by Antony. Arthur Humphreys has suggested that the Elizabethans' fascination with Rome is based on these two paradoxical aspects:

> Roman history offered some of the most impressive themes available to the Renaissance, an era when political lessons were eagerly sought in antiquity. . . . What, in general, Roman history presented was Roman arms triumphant abroad, and the Roman state stormily evolving at home. Faced in their own lands with intestine divisions, Renaissance scholars noted with awe the extent and continuity of Roman power, and with keen curiosity the contentions within Rome itself.[8]

Shakespeare's play demonstrates this thematic paradox. The heavens tremble, thunder and lightning descend, and the head of the Roman state is assassinated; nevertheless, just as in the farthest reaches of the cosmos the stars continue on their way, the Romans go on believing in themselves as a coherent and even harmonious entity. The Senate feels like this, despite its moments of panic and confusion. Even the Roman mob, fickle as it is, is fickle on behalf of what it thinks of as Rome. When it rages first against Caesar and then against Brutus, it rages from a solid stand: its conviction that it is in itself, somehow, Rome.

The members of the two groups just mentioned do not necessarily identify with each other. Casca, for example, describes the common people in uncomplimentary terms: "The rabblement howted, and clapp'd their chopp'd hands, and threw up their sweaty night-caps, and utter'd such a deal of stinking breath" (I.ii.244–246). But this vision of the Roman people does not in the least stop Casca from joining Cassius's plot to rectify the balance of what he thinks of as Rome, to bring this more aristocratic Rome back into harmony with the macrocosm-microcosm alignment between the universe and human society.

FIRE AND BLOOD

Thematic patterns of fire and blood, with their vivid imagery, are among the most immediately noticeable in the play. Sometimes they accompany each other. Cassius, having recruited Casca to the conspiracy while the storm rages, compares the weather with their new project:

> And the complexion of the element
> In favor's like the work we have in hand,
> Most bloody, fiery, and most terrible.   (I.iii.128–130)

Calphurnia's description of the same night includes a portent that is simultaneously fiery and bloody:

> Fierce fiery warriors fought upon the clouds
> In ranks and squadrons and right form of war,
> Which drizzled blood upon the Capitol.   (II.ii.19–21)

Images of blood and fire also combine in the funeral pyres of persons who have died violently. Strato, having helped Brutus commit suicide by holding Brutus's sword while Brutus ran onto it, assumes the body will be cremated: "The conquerors can but make a fire of him" (V.v.55).[9]

Earlier, Caesar's body, which Antony had just exhibited in the Forum with all its bloody wounds, is burned by the mob as it rages for revenge:

> Come, away, away!
> We'll burn his body in the holy place,
> And with the brands fire the traitors' houses.   (III.ii.253–255)

Maurice Charney has examined this passage:

The Second Plebian's cry, "Go fetch fire!" suggests that firebrands are brought in from offstage, but the mob could also ignite the firebrands right there in front of the audience. Actual fire at this hectic moment is a powerful image of the citizens' passionate and destructive temper, and there is a sense of poetic justice in the use of brands from Caesar's funeral pyre to burn the conspirators' houses. It shows the double aspect of fire: consecration and destruction. In an overall view, fire, which was first identified with the conspiracy as a symbol of destruction, has now, after the murder of Caesar, become an instrument of vengeance. It thus takes on a purgative, consecrating role.[10]

In what Charney would presumably consider its purgative aspect, fire accompanies the violence of battle; Cassius, peering nearsightedly into the haze, asks Titinius, "Are those my tents where I perceive the fire?" (V.iii.13). Fire can be a means of death, of suicide that by Roman standards might be considered honorable and purifying; Portia kills herself by swallowing fire (IV.iii.156).

Besides its thematic function in destruction and purification, fire serves other purposes in the play. To Ligarius, fire symbolizes courage. Declaring his allegiance to Brutus's cause, he says, "And with a heart new-fir'd I follow you" (II.i.332). (This image might also refer to metalworking; Ligarius has a newly made heart, so to speak.) Brutus equates fire with anger and claims to have little of it, to carry anger "as a flint bears fire / Who, much enforced, shows a hasty spark / And straight is cold again" (IV.iii.111–113). Antony, by contrast, welcomes the idea of fire as anger and deliberately fans the flames. He dares not read the will of Caesar to the people, he says, because "it will inflame you, it will make you mad" (III.ii.144).

Fire can have an orderly, utilitarian aspect. As a candle or lamp, it lights Brutus's study (II.i.7) or his tent (IV.iii.164); but even in this commonplace role, it can suddenly ally itself with the supernatural, flickering upon the entrance of Caesar's ghost (275). And a mysterious, otherworldly aspect of fire contributes to the play's suggestion that reality, like future time, is ultimately unknowable and not subject to human control. Casca describes one of the sights that has so terrified him during the storm:

> A common slave—you know him well by sight—
> Held up his left hand, which did flame and burn
> Like twenty torches join'd; and yet his hand,
> Not sensible of fire, remain'd unscorched.   (I.iii.15–18)

The storm itself is composed in large part of fire. In this way it stands out in Casca's apparently wide experience with storms: "But never till tonight, never till now, / Did I go though a tempest dropping fire" (5–10).

Like fire, blood in *Julius Caesar* sometimes appears in a practical, utilitarian aspect. It may keep to its place and course properly through people's veins. Brutus speaks of "every drop of blood / That every Roman bears" (II.i.136–137) as he explains that the conspirators do not need to swear an oath since they are certain to keep their promises anyhow. Similarly, Brutus when confirming his love for Portia envisions his own blood flowing in an orderly though gloomy manner:

> You are my true and honorable wife,
> As dear to me as are the ruddy drops
> That visit my sad heart.   (288–290)

Shortly before he is murdered, Caesar uses "blood" in this more ordinary physical sense of safely circulating and, since it is Caesar's blood, circulating in a constant and unfiery manner. The conspirators, as a pretext for gathering around Caesar, are begging him to repeal the banishment of Metellus Cimber's brother. Caesar responds:

> I must prevent thee, Cimber.
> These couchings and these lowly courtesies
> Might fire the blood of ordinary men . . .
>   . . . Be not fond
> To think that Caesar bears such rebel blood.   (III.i.35–40)

Within a few lines, Caesar's blood is no longer under the control of Caesar but has burst out of bounds and is all over the stage, creating horrible visions literally and rhetorically. This is the more usual function of blood in this play. The words "blood" or "bloody" occur thirty-six times in the text, almost always in a context of violence. References to wounds, cuts, stabs, carvings, and hewings total seventeen, not counting stage directions or less literal locutions such as Casca's "Speak, hands, for me" (III.i.75). Even inanimate objects are affected. Blood spouts from Caesar's statue in Calphurnia's dream (II.ii.76–79), and runs from Pompey's statue during the assassination, at least as reported by Antony (III.ii.189).

Caesar's actual blood flows in sufficient quantity to supply his killers with material for the next ritual, to be orchestrated by Brutus:

> Stoop, Romans, stoop,
> And let us bathe our hands in Caesar's blood
> Up to the elbows, and besmear our swords.   (III.i.105–107)

It is these bloodied hands that Antony shakes when he enters and declares himself ready to share Caesar's fate: "I know not, gentlemen, what you intend, / Who else must be let blood" (151–152). Brutus's reply, which links imagery of blood and fire, is that Caesar's blood is not really blood, or is, perhaps, merely a superficial and less important aspect of the situation:

> Though now we must appear bloody and cruel,
> As by our hands and this our present act
> You see we do, yet see you but our hands,
> And this the bleeding business they have done.

> Our hearts you see not, they are pitiful [full of pity];
> And pity to the general wrong of Rome—
> As fire drives out fire, so pity pity—
> Have done this deed on Caesar.   (165–172)

This is not a new concept for Brutus. He has consoled himself previously with the claim that this murder is in so good a cause that it does not count as murder, blood or no blood, and that if properly done, the murder will reflect this high-minded ideal:

> We all stand up against the spirit of Caesar,
> And in the spirit of men there is no blood;
> O that we then could come by Caesar's spirit
> And not dismember Caesar! But, alas,
> Caesar must bleed for it! And, gentle friends,
> Let's kill him boldly, but not wrathfully;
> Let's carve him as a dish fit for the gods,
> Not hew him as a carcass fit for hounds.   (II.i.166–174)

This wistful directive is not followed in the least, and the brutality of Caesar's murder is the more obvious because of the contrast.

Antony, not surprisingly, sees the blood in a different light. "O pardon me, thou bleeding piece of earth," he says to the corpse of Caesar, "That I am meek and gentle with these butchers" (III.i.254–255). Caesar's wounds become in Antony's view "dumb mouths," which "do ope their ruby lips / To beg the voice and utterance of my tongue." Antony then envisions a world of violence; "blood and destruction" will become the norm, and Caesar's spirit (which Brutus had thought he could "get at") will wreak revenge.

In Antony's funeral speech, blood provides the culminating image. Caesar's bloody mantle, the rents made by the assassins' daggers, and finally the wounds themselves achieve their rhetorical goals. Antony returns to the image of the wounds as mouths:

> I tell you that which you yourselves do know,
> Show you sweet Caesar's wounds, poor, poor dumb mouths,
> And bid them speak for me.   (III.ii.224–226)

Were he himself a better orator, Antony says modestly, he might "put a tongue / In every wound of Caesar, that should move / The stones of Rome to rise and mutiny" (227–230).

G. Wilson Knight has pointed out the many images associating Caesar's blood with richness: "It is, as it were, a life-stream of infinite value. . . . It is thus recognized by Antony and the conspirators who bathe in it as in a stream of life, emblematic of fortune."[11] The theme of order and hierarchy in the cosmos here overlaps with the themes of blood and fire, combining destruction with purification; Caesar as the greatest man in the world is at the top of his segment of the chain of being.

Leo Kirschbaum has taken a more literal look at blood in *Julius Caesar*, considering the actual (or, rather, the fake) blood used onstage as an image in itself. The Elizabethans were thoroughly accustomed to stage gore. "Spectacular blood effects were created by painting, smearing, or sprinkling and by concealed bladders, sponges, and animal entrails."[12] Kirschbaum feels that Shakespeare intended for Caesar's murder to be exploited in the audience's view, with maximum shock value. Thus, the theme of order and disorder is demonstrated through the brutality of the murder:

> That the dignified and gentle Brutus should propose the ghastly procedure of the conspirators bathing their hands in the blood of Caesar's body wrenches the mind. It emphasizes the disorder in the man. The major lesson of Shakespeare's history plays is so simple that its tremendous significance may be overlooked. It is this: *History is made by men.*[13]

RELIGION, PORTENTS, AND DREAMS

From our perspective, Roman religion may well seem akin to, if not identical with, sheer superstition. (This kinship is probably easier to see in other people's religions than in one's own.) However, as *Julius Caesar* shows, Roman religion was not uniform, and not everyone participated in its more superstitious aspects. One could choose among a variety of philosophical worldviews, some of which included the recognition of traditional gods and the observance of sacrifices and other rituals, and some of which did not.

By the first century B.C., Rome's religious heritage was something of a potpourri. Among the ingredients were the ancient festivals left over from the small farming and herding community Rome had once been; the Lupercal was one of these. Rome had also picked up the Greek gods and goddesses, giving them Roman names and often identifying them with abstract concepts to a greater degree than the Greeks had done. Various types of priests performed various types of duties. The flamens, for example, were attached to temples and performed daily sacrifices. Ordinarily they were not allowed to hold public office. The pontifices, by contrast, could hold public office and were especially responsible for the calendar, determining the dates of festivals and influencing state decisions of many sorts. Julius Caesar held the office of *pontifex maximus,* along with his other offices, and was thus Rome's highest-ranking priest. His project of reforming the calendar was conveniently aligned with the pontifices' specialty.

Most of the emphasis in Roman religion fell on performing rituals to propitiate the gods and foretell the future, with a practical emphasis on the here and now. Essentially the process was one of bargaining. If a god were pleased with the sacrifice offered, he or she would hear the worshipper's request; if not, the worshipper might simply try another god. The question of an afterlife seems not to have interested the Romans, although they had a vague belief that a man's spirit might survive him. Burial rites were nevertheless considered very important, whether the corpse was interred or cremated.

In the traditional Roman view, dreams and omens represented messages from the gods. These should be interpreted by priests, if possible, as authorities on such matters, although the private person who dreamed the dream or noticed the omen would naturally do his best to understand it. This was the traditional view; by the first century B.C., many sophisticated Romans tended to downplay such assumptions. Stoicism, a school of thought developed by the Greek philosopher Zeno in the fourth century B.C., appealed to many Romans. Cicero professed and wrote about it, and Brutus was clearly influenced by its emphasis on logic, civic duty, and indifference to the superficial vicissitudes of life. If one did not care what fortune brought one's way, presumably there was no point in interpreting omens to find out the details. Even more oblivious to the supernatural, in fact directly opposed to belief in it, were the Epicureans, followers of another Greek philosopher who felt that wisdom should be sought by plain living and attending to the evidence of the senses. Shakespeare's Cassius is attracted to this view, although, as we will see, he has doubts.

At the same time that they questioned the credibility of omens and sacrifices, even educated and sophisticated Romans supported religious observances—festivals in particular—for their patriotic value. Festivals were thought to nurture a sense of community and history. Thus, Caesar, who likes to think of himself as above mere portents, nevertheless leads a procession on the feast of the Lupercal and orders those in charge to "leave no ceremony out" (I.ii.11).

Supernatural Signs: Believers and Doubters

The number of characters who scoff at omens in *Julius Caesar* is rather large, although, interestingly, many of them waver in their disbelief. Caesar, for example, in the scene mentioned just previously, refuses to listen to the Soothsayer: "He is a dreamer, let us leave him" (24). Yet a short time afterward Cassius remarks:

> For he [Caesar] is superstitious grown of late,
> Quite from the main opinion he held once,
> Of fantasy, of dreams, and ceremonies.   (II.i.195–197)

When we next see Caesar, he is sending an order to his household augurers—a class of priests who specialized in interpreting auspices, or ceremonies undertaken to find out if the gods approved some specific enterprise. Caesar cannot decide whether to go to the Capitol that morning, and he asks his priests to "do present [immediate] sacrifice, / And bring me their opinions of success" (II.ii.5–6). This method of divination involved examining the entrails of a sacrificed animal (usually a sheep or a pig). In this case, the priests send a dramatic reply:

> They would not have you to stir forth today.
> Plucking the entrails of an offering forth,
> They could not find a heart within the beast.   (38–40)

Interpretation of omens, of course, is always a subjective matter, and Caesar substitutes his own opinion:

> The gods do this in shame of cowardice.
> Caesar should be a beast without a heart
> If he should stay at home today for fear.   (41–43)

Interpretation also overrules the obvious message in Calphurnia's dream of Caesar's statue spouting blood, "like a fountain with an hundred spouts"; Decius Brutus claims the dream is about the "reviving blood" that Caesar's leadership bestows on Rome (77, 88). So despite the Soothsayer's message, the storm with its plentitude of portents, Calphurnia's dream, and the heartless beast, Caesar sets out for the Capitol on the Ides of March.

Cassius, who presents himself as a matter-of-fact person and talks Casca out of his fear of the storm, later begins to regard omens in a different light. As he prepares to fight the battle of Philippi, he tells Messala:

> You know I once held Epicurus strong,
> And his opinion; now I change my mind,
> And partly credit things that do presage.   (V.i.76–78)

Cassius then explains that his army, while on the march, had been accompanied by "two mighty eagles," which perched on their leading banners and took food from the soldiers' hands. Since the eagle was a symbol of Rome and a high-ranking bird in the hierarchical order of creation, this visitation was seen in a positive light. But now the omen has changed:

> This morning are they fled away and gone,
> And in their steads do ravens, crows, and kites
> Fly o'er our heads, and downward look on us
> As we were sickly prey. Their shadows seem
> A canopy most fatal, under which
> Our army lies, ready to give up the ghost.   (83–88)

This lengthy description is as unlike the brisk Cassius as is the sentiment he expresses. He is able to talk himself out of the mood—"I but believe it partly"—but the prophecy is, of course, accurate.

The pattern we see is that in this play, those who disbelieve omens come to grief. Is Shakespeare suggesting that superstitions are in fact correct? (A substantial portion of his audience might have nodded in agreement.) Or is he simply using effective dramatic devices?

Calphurnia, we remember, believed in the warning power of her dream even though, as she tells Caesar, she is not ordinarily superstitious: "I never stood on ceremonies" (II.ii.13). It is not her fault that she is overruled. She has done her best. Another dreamer, however, Cinna the Poet, disobeys the warning of his dream even though he is capable of figuring it out:

> I dreamt tonight that I did feast with Caesar,
> And things unluckily charge my fantasy.
> I have no will to wander forth of doors,
> Yet something leads me forth.   (III.iii.1–4)

The time pattern is a bit confusing here. By "tonight," Cinna presumably means the previous night, since Caesar has been killed in the meantime and Antony has incited the mob to riot. Possibly, however, the hour is quite late, the mob is still rioting, and Cinna has been asleep but has awoken and wandered forth of doors. In either case, since all Rome knows that Caesar is dead, Cinna would know it as well, and "feasting with Caesar" would take on an overtone of sharing his fate rather than his hospitality. Nevertheless, like Caesar, he chooses to ignore supernatural warnings and to leave a place of safety for one of danger.

Marjorie Garber has commented on the frequency with which such warnings occur in vain:

> The play is full of omens and portents, augury and dreams, and almost without exception these omens are misinterpreted. . . . *Julius Caesar* is not only a political play, but also a play of character. Its imagery of dream and sign, an imagery so powerful that it enters the plot on the level of action, is a means of examining character and consciousness.[14]

Brutus, according to Garber, is "the least self-aware" of the characters, "because he thinks of himself as a supremely rational man." He is subject to insomnia (II.i.61–62), and the ghost of Caesar "seems to come from the dream state." Brutus's guilt for killing Caesar, which he will not consciously acknowledge because he is determined to believe he did the only right thing, has evoked the ghost. Garber continues: "*Julius Caesar* is a complex and ambiguous play, which does not concern itself principally with political theory, but with the strange blindness of the rational mind—in politics and elsewhere—to the great irrational powers which flow through life and control it."[15]

Tradition and Religious Ritual: The Feast of the Lupercal

Naomi Conn Liebler has investigated the relationship between *Julius Caesar* and the traditional Lupercalian festival, which Shakespeare might have read about in another of Plutarch's lives, that of Romulus, legendary founder of Rome. (North's translation was published as one large volume, and Shakespeare would have had all the biographies conveniently at hand.) The life of Romulus gives "a substantive account of the festival, its history and implication, and some hint of its actual as well as its metaphoric relation to the last days of Julius Caesar."[16] Although Shakespeare does not borrow specific incidents or phrases from *Romulus*, as he does from the biographies more closely connected with his play, he does borrow at least one image, that of blood dropping from the heavens, one of the portents Calphurnia reports of the storm-troubled night preceding the Ides of March.[17]

The Lupercal was traditionally a festival of fertility and purgation, intended to ensure the fruitfulness of the land and the increase of the flocks. By analogy, it was also expected to renew the vigor, physical and moral, of both the individual and the state. To begin the festival, priests sacrificed goats and cut strips from the goats' skins; a group of boys or men (originally only two) then took the strips and ran through the city, striking anyone who stood in their path. Such a ritual blow was thought to restore fertility, as Caesar points out:

> . . . for our elders say
> The barren, touched in this holy chase,
> Shake off their sterile curse.   (I.ii.7–9)

Images of barrenness and sterility, Liebler points out, appear throughout the play. Murellus, for example, warns the people of dire consequences if they forget their admiration of Pompey:

> Run to your houses, fall upon your knees,
> Pray to the gods to intermit the plague
> That needs must light on this ingratitude.   (I.i.53–55)

Elsewhere people are ill—Caius Ligarius, for example; they are deaf, sleepless, troubled at heart, disturbed by dreams and portents. Liebler points out Plutarch's description of events following Caesar's death: a comet appeared, the sun was dimmed and gave little heat, and the crops rotted in the ground before they could ripen. According to Liebler, "These are doomsday images of the horror of sterility that threatens the welfare of any essentially agrarian state. They suggest the Waste Land against which purgation and fertility rituals such as the Lupercalia were invented."[18]

Similar folk customs, according to Liebler, could be found in Elizabethan England. Among the rituals Shakespeare would have known were the "beating of the bounds," a curious tradition in which the location of the parish boundaries was impressed upon young boys by being walked along these boundaries and beaten with willow wands. Morris dancing, in one version of which a character called the Fool tries to whip the spectators, is also analogous to the Lupercalian race. According to Liebler,

> Certain features of the festivals celebrated by both urban and rural Eliza-
> bethans offer tantalizing prospects for any of the following suppositions: that
> *Julius Caesar*'s incorporation of Lupercalian elements would have struck fa-

miliar chords for its audience; that the play's concerns with right rule and
order, and their passage, are essentially the same as those of many folk and
civic festivals generally; that Shakespeare's familiarity with the rural practices
of various festivals in Warwickshire sensitized him to the analogous rites he
read about in Plutarch.[19]

These connections can be seen as an example of the way universal themes can
function in literature, forming a bridge between the experience of the characters in
the play and the playgoers in Shakespeare's audience. The idea of ancient ritual as
a way to influence the future and thus avert disaster would seem to run very deep
indeed.

Julius Caesar and Christian Controversy

David Kaula has pointed out numerous Christian analogies in *Julius Caesar*, including such passing references as the reaction of the Roman populace to Caesar's
murder: "Men, wives, and children stare, cry out, and run, / As it were doomsday"
(III.i.97–98). Doomsday would not have been a familiar concept in Roman religion, concerned as it was with the here and now rather than with any far-reaching
apocalyptic view of the future.

More specifically, in Kaula's view, the play presents a variety of analogies with
the religious controversies of Shakespeare's day. Cassius, persuading Brutus to
join the conspiracy, resembles a radical Protestant: "Cassius's . . . vision of Caesar
as the prodigious, terrifying figure who thunders, lightens, opens graves, and
roars like a lion also reveals a number of analogies to the Protestant polemics
against the Pope."[20] Since the pope was identified by many English Protestants
with the Anti-Christ of the Book of Revelation, Cassius's description of Caesar as
disproportionately large and blustery, "grotesquely inflated," would cover this
figure as well.

Antony, certainly no Puritan with his love of music and theater, picks up in this
analogy the opposite religious extreme. As Catholics were expected to do, he puts
emphasis on sacred relics. He tells the crowd in his Forum speech:

> Let but the commons hear this testament—
> Which, pardon me, I do not mean to read—
> And they would go and kiss dead Caesar's wounds,
> And dip their napkins in his sacred blood;
> Yea, beg a hair of him for memory.   (III.ii.130–134)

According to Kaula, "Antony is describing something that members of Shakespeare's audience could have witnessed in their own city: the avid quest for relics
by the followers of Catholic missionary priests executed at Tyburn."[21] (The reader
might also assume, within the earlier analogy, that if Cassius has presented Caesar
as the Anti-Christ, Antony is here presenting him as Christ.)

It would be "convenient, or schematically satisfying," Kaula remarks, to find "somewhere in the play a man between the two extremes, an Anglican *via media*." Brutus becomes a possibility here; he takes a more balanced view of Caesar than either Cassius or Antony, admiring him even while he plots to kill him. But, Kaula concludes, Shakespeare cannot portray an Anglican Brutus on the English stage; "he is, after all, a regicide." Instead, Kaula suggests, "In Brutus, Shakespeare shows the misapplication of religious ideas, not in Cassius's or Antony's propagandistic fashion, but in a sincere if misconceived attempt to restore the one-time brotherhood of free Romans."[22]

In short, according to Kaula, "If *Julius Caesar* can be tentatively seen as reflecting Shakespeare's own religious attitudes, it would seem to indicate considerable skepticism on his part toward the more extreme religious tendencies of the period, both Protestant and Catholic—a conviction that such tendencies jeopardized that ideal of spiritual fellowship which is more fundamental, more essentially Christian, than particular doctrinal or sectarian commitments."[23]

THEMATIC HIERARCHIES: MAN AND THE ANIMAL KINGDOM

An orderly hierarchy of animals was part of the traditional pattern of creation as envisioned by the Elizabethans, although the exact sequence of this retinue did not always agree; sometimes the elephant was described as king of beasts, and sometimes (more often) the lion. Of birds, the eagle was almost always given precedence.[24] Man occupies the top rung of the animal ladder, but he has only one foot on it, the other reaching up toward the angelic rungs. Man, according to Psalms 8:5, was created "a little lower than the angels."[25] Man's special faculties—reason, for example, and spiritual awareness—are what keep us at the top. Should we fail to exercise these gifts, according to traditional ideas, we would slip down the chain into some more bestial category. (It should be noted that animals are not in themselves seen as imperfect parts of creation just because they occupy lower links on the chain. Each animal—and, for that matter, each plant or mineral—was seen as having its own kind of perfection. To exercise this perfection, however, each component of the chain must stay in its place. A man who behaves like a giraffe—just to invent a fanciful example—is violating the chain of being, but there is nothing wrong with an actual giraffe.)

In practice, the clarity and order of the chain of being often seemed to get itself tangled. We have already mentioned the lion-versus-elephant ambiguity. The idea of the four elements, the basic building blocks of creation, also harbors paradoxes. Listed in order, from top to bottom, these would be fire, air, water, and earth; the animal kingdom was often ranked according to which of these elements the animal in question occupied. (A fish would outrank a mole presumably.) Yet traditional medical theories held that in a healthy organism, the elements should be balanced, without any one of them predominating. Perhaps we might conclude that the idea of the fixed and orderly chain of being was valued as a symbolic entity more than actually used as a large-scale categorical system.

In *Julius Caesar*, many references to animals are similes or other comparisons, but others are the actual creatures themselves. Besides numerous symbolic animals, some related to the medieval bestiary traditions and others involved in augury, the play mentions some practical everyday animals, just doing their jobs, and under the control of man as the Bible stipulates.[26]

The birds that Cassius notices accompanying his army are actual birds, within the narrative universe of *Julius Caesar*, yet they also function as symbolic portents. The eagle, emblem of Rome and king of the birds, is replaced by low-ranking scavengers that cast ominous shadows as they circle above their future snacks (V.i.79–88). Earlier, the "bird of night," the owl, who sat "even at noonday upon the marketplace, / Howting and shrieking" (I.iii.27–28), has a similar function. In some contexts, the owl can symbolize wisdom, but this one has simply departed from its usual nocturnal habits and thus signifies disorder.

Fantasy animals, reminiscent of the medieval bestiaries and their moralizations, appear in Decius Brutus's description of the tales he tells to Caesar:

> . . . he loves to hear
> That unicorns may be betray'd with trees,
> And bears with glasses, elephants with holes,
> Lions with toils, and men with flatterers.   (II.i.203–206)

These curious practices might have been familiar to Shakespeare's audience, in folklore if not in actual experience, but could use explanation today. To "betray," or capture, a unicorn, one stands in front of a tree while the unicorn charges, then steps quickly aside so that the unicorn drives his horn into the tree trunk. The glass used for catching bears is a looking glass; the bear, proverbially vain, will stop to admire itself. One induces elephants to walk over covered pits, and drops a net over lions.

Caesar and the Animal Kingdom

Much of the play's animal imagery focuses on Caesar, and a given image is positive or negative according to the emotions of the speaker. Caesar compares himself to a lion, traditionally kingly, and brother to another lion upon whom Caesar has grafted a personification of Danger:

> Danger knows full well
> That Caesar is more dangerous than he.
> We are two lions litter'd in one day,
> And I the elder and more terrible.   (II.ii.44–47)

Cassius also compares Caesar to a lion, but this one is a ravaging predator and not a natural sovereign. To reinforce the parallel, Cassius brings in a wolf as well, and here, too, the context is important, for wolves (as nurturers of Romulus and Remus) sometimes function as a positive symbol of Rome. Here, however, both predators are negative:

> . . . I know he [Caesar] would not be a wolf,
> But that he sees the Romans are but sheep;
> He were no lion, were not Romans hinds.   (I.iii.104–106)

(A hind is a female deer.)

Meanwhile, Rome does have some actual lions that become symbols of disorder during the storm on the night of March 14. One of these meets Casca in the street, looks at him, and "went surly by / Without annoying me" (I.iii.21–22). Another has "whelped in the streets" (II.ii.17). Another of the lions Cassius used as a symbol for Caesar is "the lion in the Capitol," apparently a real lion, which Shakespeare envisions as a sort of mascot.[27]

Another potentially kingly image of Caesar becomes in context a negative one as Flavius compares Caesar to a high-flying bird, one who has climbed out of his assigned altitude and thus violated the chain of being. Flavius urges Murellus to continue trying to suppress the people's enthusiasm for Caesar:

> These growing feathers pluck'd from Caesar's wing
> Will make him fly an ordinary pitch,
> Who else would soar above the view of man
> And keep us all in servile fearfulness.   (I.i.72–75)

Brutus's view of Caesar invokes animal imagery so negative as to become satanic. Caesar, he admits to himself, has not yet done anything really terrible, but perhaps he has been lying low, a snake in the grass, and waiting for an opportunity: "It is the bright day that brings forth the adder" (II.i.14). The snake has been traditionally associated with Satan, as we see in the Bible's account of the Fall: "Now the serpent was more subtil [*sic*] than any beast of the field."[28] Brutus's rationalization for killing Caesar, not very convincing if viewed as a piece of logic, gains power from its imagaic resonance:

> Fashion it thus; that what he is, augmented,
> Would run to these and these extremities;
> And therefore think him as a serpent's egg,
> Which, hatch'd, would as his kind grow mischievous,
> And kill him in the shell.   (30–34)

Once Caesar is dead, his animal parallels shift from predator to prey. Antony compares him to a deer pursued and finally slain by hunters, with a series of puns on "hart" (a male deer):

> Here wast thou bay'd, brave hart,
> Here didst thou fall, and here thy hunters stand,
> Sign'd in thy spoil, and crimson'd in thy lethe.
> O world! Thou wast the forest to this hart,
> And this indeed, O world, the heart of thee.

> How like a deer, strooken by many princes,
> Dost thou here lie!   (III.i.204–210)

To "bay" an animal is to pursue it until it turns (with its back to a boulder or tree if it can manage) to make a final stand. "Sign'd in thy spoil, and crimson'd in thy lethe" refers to the blood of the slain animal, ritually daubed upon the hunters; Caesar's murderers have just bathed their hands in his blood. The imagery focuses sympathetically on Caesar until Antony suddenly remembers that he must be "meek and gentle with these butchers" (255) if he hopes to get their permission to speak at the funeral. He then enlarges his imagaic picture into a royal hunt, of the sort Shakespeare's audience may have seen depicted on tapestries, and refers to the killers as if they were heroic noblemen, "many princes."

Horses and Dogs

Mixed in with the symbolic and heraldic animals of *Julius Caesar* are numerous more ordinary creatures, going about their business, metaphorically or literally, and directed in their actions by their human owners. Again, the connotations are positive or negative according to the context.

When Antony grumbles about Lepidus's unfitness for high office and Octavius then praises him as "a tried and valiant soldier," Antony replies:

> So is my horse, Octavius, and for that
> I do appoint him store of provender.
> It is a creature that I teach to fight,
> To wind, to stop, to run directly on,
> His corporeal motion govern'd by my spirit.   (IV.i.29–33)

This sounds like a very good horse, but the analogy is not a compliment, since a man is theoretically higher than a horse on the chain of being. Yet it is still a step up for poor Lepidus; a few lines earlier, Antony has compared him to a considerably lower-ranking member of the equine section of the chain:

> And though we lay these honors on this man
> To ease ourselves of diverse sland'rous loads,
> He shall but bear them as the ass bears gold,
> To groan and sweat under the business,
> Either led or driven, as we point the way;
> And having brought our treasure where we will,
> Then take we down his load, and turn him off
> (Like to the empty ass) to shake his ears
> And graze in commons.   (19–27)

Horses (and asses) in *Julius Caesar* partake generally of a pattern of order, doing man's will, though sometimes reluctantly. "Horses did neigh" during the storm preceding the Ides of March (II.ii.23), adding to the atmosphere of disorderly ruckus, but with so many astonishing things going on it would be odd if they did not. Brutus, when he feels that Cassius is no longer as devoted a friend as he used to be, describes him as a horse who pretends to be keen on his work but actually is not:

> But hollow men, like horses hot at hand,
> Make gallant show and promise of their mettle;
> But when they should endure the bloody spur,
> They fall their crests, and like deceitful jades
> Sink in the trial.   (IV.ii.22–27)

Dogs, too, actual or metaphorical, do what is expected of them in *Julius Caesar*, though the positive or negative connotations of dog imagery often reflect the speaker's apparent attitude toward dogs. The "dogs of war" that Antony proposes to let slip (III.i.273) are presumably ferocious creatures, but they are simply doing what they have been trained to do when let off their leash.

Other dog images are downright disparaging. Caroline Spurgeon, a pioneer in the analysis of Shakespeare's imagery, has noted several clusters of images occurring throughout Shakespeare's work, one of which includes dogs: "Whenever the idea . . . of false friends or flatterers occurs, we find a rather curious set of images which play around it. These are: a dog or spaniel, fawning and licking; candy, sugar, or sweets, thawing, or melting."[29]

Julius Caesar provides an example of this cluster. The conspirators have gathered around Caesar, on the pretense of persuading him to repeal the banishment of Metellus Cimber's brother. Caesar, speaking of himself as usual in the third person, is greatly annoyed. Words illustrating Spurgeon's image cluster are here italicized:

> Be not fond [foolish]
> To think that Caesar bears such rebel blood
> That will be *thaw'd* from the true quality
> With that which *melteth* fools—I mean *sweet* words,
> Low-crooked curtsies, and *base spaniel fawning*.
> Thy brother by decree is banished;
> If thou dost bend, and pray, and *fawn* for him,
> I spurn thee like a *cur* out of my way.   (III.i.39–46)

The image of fawning dogs recurs, preceded by an image of a melting, or in this case semiliquid, kind of sweetness. Before the battle of Philippi, Cassius taunts Antony for his verbal eloquence:

> Antony,
> The posture of your blows is yet unknown;
> But for your words, they rob the Hybla bees
> And leave them honeyless.   (V.i.32–35)

(Hybla, in Sicily, was noted for its honey.) Antony replies by reminding Cassius and Brutus of their hypocritical behavior at the time of the murder. In this instance, the imagery clearly links hypocrisy, or flattery, with the theme of disorder and the misfortunes that result when man abandons his place on the chain of being:

> You showed your teeth like apes, and fawn'd like hounds,
> And bow'd like bondmen, kissing Caesar's feet;
> Whilst damned Casca, like a cur, behind
> Strook Caesar on the neck. O you flatterers!   (41–44)

Animals, Brutus, and the Chain of Being

Apes do not seem to be a standard part of the image cluster Spurgeon has described, but in the passage just quoted, they fit into the overall idea. One imagines the flash of an insincere grimace. Apes also resemble humans, and in this simile the resemblance is disturbing, since apes are nonetheless animals. In behaving like apes, the conspirators have definitely slipped down a few links in the chain of being.

Antony makes a similar use of animal imagery in his Forum speech, implicitly comparing man, possessed of reason and judgment, with animals without these faculties:

> O judgment! thou art fled to brutish beasts,
> And men have lost their reason.   (III.ii.104–105)

That "brutish" is here a pun on "Brutus" has been proposed by numerous scholars and is a natural association that the readers, or audience members, are likely to make on their own.[30] The construction of Antony's speech supports this interpretation. Antony has been demonstrating that Brutus's announced motive for killing Caesar, Caesar's ambition, is not a reasonable one, since Caesar was not ambitious. If Brutus is not reasonable, not even a man, if he is a brutish beast, then the murder becomes an even more extreme violation of the principle of orderly hierarchy.

But at the end of the play, Antony does a strange about-face with this image, returning Brutus not only to the human segment of the chain of being but to a high position on that segment. Even the idea of the proper balance of the elements comes into the picture:

> This was the noblest Roman of them all.
> All the conspirators, save only he,
> Did that they did in envy of great Caesar;
> He, only in a general honest thought
> And common good to all, made one of them.
> His life was gentle, and the elements
> So mix'd in him that Nature might stand up
> And say to all the world, "This was a man!"   (V.v.68–75)

Antony's complex character might supply all sorts of reasons for this change of heart or, at any rate, change of publicly professed evaluation. History comes into the situation as well; according to Plutarch, Antony had often said that Brutus had the purest motives of the assassins.[31] We are also aware that this is the end of the play. Here resounding statements contribute to a sense of closure. Brutus's reinstatement on the chain of being does fulfill this function while it leaves undisturbed the more ambiguous and less closable components of the action, such as the relationship between Antony and Octavius, which Shakespeare will need to develop when he returns to ancient Rome with *Antony and Cleopatra*.

NOTES

1. Northrop Frye, *Fools of Time: Studies in Shakespearean Tragedy* (Toronto: University of Toronto Press, 1967), p. 3. Frye's discussion covers a wide range, drawing examples from the literature of many periods and cultures, and does not pursue a specific connection with *Julius Caesar*.

2. Frye has suggested that comedy, as opposed to tragedy, emphasizes the cyclical, seasonal, recurring aspect of time. In comedy one may be granted a second chance. Consequences are not so irrevocable after all, and people thought to be dead reappear in the last act. See *Anatomy of Criticism: Four Essays* (Princeton, N.J.: Princeton University Press, 1957), pp. 158–171, 183–185, 203–206.

3. Sigurd Burckhardt, "How Not to Murder Caesar," in Burckhardt, *Shakespearean Meanings* (Princeton, N.J.: Princeton University Press, 1968), pp. 3–21.

4. Ibid., p. 5. The quotations immediately following this one occur on pp. 5–6.

5. Ibid., p. 9.

6. Two Englishmen, Isaac Newton (1643–1727) and Edmund Halley (1656–1742), were leaders in solving the riddle of the comets. Halley's comet, named after its discoverer, had caused great dread in its earlier and more mysterious visits. Calculations have identified it with the comet seen in 1066, identified in the popular imagination with William the Conqueror's victory at the battle of Hastings.

7. Scientific Elizabethans knew that the earth-centered Ptolemaic universe was an outdated concept. Copernicus's treatise on the revolution of the celestial spheres had been published in 1543; in the early seventeenth century, the work of Kepler and Galileo, respectively, would set the planets spinning round the sun. But the old concept persisted in the popular imagination and as a poetic image. See E. B. Knobel, "Astronomy and Astrology," in C. T. Onions, ed., *Shakespeare's England: An Account of the Life and Manners of His Age* (Oxford: Clarendon Press, 1916, 1966), vol. 1, pp. 444–461.

8. Arthur Humphreys, Introduction to *Julius Caesar* (Oxford: Oxford University Press, 1994), p. 30.

9. Cremation was the usual means of disposal of the dead in Rome at this time, although interment was also practiced. See "Burial and Cremation," in Paul Harvey, ed., *The Oxford Companion to Classical Literature* (Oxford: Clarendon Press, 1937, 1955).

10. Maurice Charney, *Shakespeare's Roman Plays: The Function of Imagery in the Drama* (Cambridge, Mass.: Harvard University Press, 1961), pp. 64–65.

11. G. Wilson Knight, *The Imperial Theme: Further Interpretations of Shakespeare's Tragedies Including the Roman Plays* (London: Oxford University Press, 1931, 1939), p. 47.

12. Leo Kirschbaum, "Shakespeare's Stage Blood and Its Critical Significance," in Leonard F. Dean, ed., *Twentieth Century Interpretations of Julius Caesar: A Collection of Critical Essays* (Englewood Cliffs, N.J.: Prentice-Hall, 1968), p. 27.

13. Ibid., pp. 34–35.

14. Marjorie Garber, *Dream in Shakespeare: From Metaphor to Metamorphosis* (New Haven, Conn.: Yale University Press, 1974), p. 48.

15. Ibid., pp. 57–58.

16. Naomi Conn Liebler, " 'Thou Bleeding Piece of Earth': The Ritual Ground of *Julius Caesar*," *ShStud* 14 (1981), 176.

17. Ibid., pp. 177–178.

18. Ibid., p. 178.

19. Ibid., p. 189.

20. David Kaula, " 'Let Us Be Sacrificers': Religious Motifs in *Julius Caesar*," *ShStud*, 14 (1981), 201.

21. Ibid., p. 205.

22. Ibid., p. 210.

23. Ibid., p. 211.

24. E.M.W. Tillyard's *The Elizabethan World Picture* (London: Chatto and Windus, 1943, 1952), though in recent years accused of oversimplification, gives an overall view of this harmonious mind-set. Tillyard quotes Elizabethan writers and also traces the classical origins of the concepts. The notion of a chain of being, according to Tillyard, began with Plato's *Timaeus* and was developed by Aristotle (p. 24).

25. King James Version (1607). The Geneva Bible (1560), apparently less concerned with the details of hierarchy, says, "a little lower than God," as do several modern versions. The meaning is usually taken to be "a little less than divine," but at the top of the scale of earthly creation nevertheless.

26. The King James Version's Genesis 1:26 gives man dominion over fish, fowl, cattle, and "every creeping thing that creepeth upon the earth." The Geneva Bible uses the phrase "rule over," but the message is the same.

27. T. S. Dorsch, in his Arden edition of *Julius Caesar*, cites Aldis Wright on this line. Wright "suggests that Shakespeare may have had in mind the lions kept in the Tower which were one of the sights of London, and to which there were many contemporary references" (p. 28).

28. Genesis 3:1. The King James Version and the Geneva Bible agree on the wording here.

29. Caroline Spurgeon, *Shakespeare's Imagery and What It Tells Us* (Cambridge: Cambridge University Press, 1935, 1966), p. 195.

30. Marvin Spevack, commenting on this line in his New Cambridge edition of *Julius Caesar*, agrees with the possibility of a pun in this context and emphasizes the Latin meaning of the word "brutus": "dull, without reason."

31. See T.B.J. Spencer, ed., *Shakespeare's Plutarch* (Harmondsworth: Penguin, 1964), p. 140.

5

CRITICAL APPROACHES

Julius Caesar was first performed in 1599 and ever since has attracted attention, on the stage and the page. Not surprisingly, the history of its criticism is a long one. Readers interested in a thorough survey of these critical works from the earliest times into the 1980s may profitably consult the reference set *Shakespearean Criticism: Excerpts from the Criticism of William Shakespeare's Plays and Poetry, from the First Published Appraisals to Current Evaluations*, ed. Mark W. Scott (Detroit, Mich.: Gale Research Co., 1988). Volume 7, pp. 138–366, is devoted to excerpts from criticism of *Julius Caesar*, chronologically arranged. The index in Volume 23 leads to additional discussions of this play in conjunction with other of Shakespeare's works.

RECENT SHAKESPEAREAN CRITICISM AND ITS TRIBUTARIES

This chapter will deal mainly with comparatively recent critical work—since the earlier twentieth century. It will touch in particular on critical approaches to *Julius Caesar* in which Shakespeare's play is found to be aligned with, or related to, one or more of the many theories that have been applied to literature but have their origins in other fields of scholarly inquiry. Philosophy, psychology, linguistics, economics, history, and sociology are among these contributing fields.

These combinational approaches are typical of recent work but have not replaced other directions of inquiry into Shakespeare—directions that, because of their more immediate accessibility to students of *Julius Caesar*, are mentioned elsewhere in this book. This mentioned-elsewhere category includes textual scholarship, studies of theme and imagery, theater history, and the kind of close reading associated with formalism or the new criticism of the 1930s and 1940s. This last approach has made useful contributions to the critical movements of the past few decades, including those discussed in this chapter, through its insistence on close analytical reading of the text.

Among the thinkers frequently invoked in twentieth-century Shakespearean criticism are sociologist and economist Karl Marx (1818–1883), psychoanalyst Sigmund Freud (1856–1939), linguist Ferdinand de Saussure (1857–1913), psychologist C. G. Jung (1875–1961), and philosopher Mikhail Bakhtin (1895–1975). Later influences include psychoanalyst Jacques Lacan (1901–1981), anthropologist Claude Lévi-Strauss (b. 1908), linguist Roland Barthes (1915–1980), philosopher Louis Althusser (1918–1990), historian Michel Foucault (1926–1984), and philosopher Jacques Derrida (b. 1930). Recent trends in Shakespearean criticism, many of which incorporate the ideas of these thinkers, have been discussed in separate articles by Terence Hawkes and Jonathan Dollimore.[1]

Heather Dubrow has provided both a general view of twentieth-century Shakespearean criticism and a specific focus on work since 1970 in the second edition (1997) of the *Riverside Shakespeare* (Boston: Houghton Mifflin), pp. 27–54. Dubrow points out that Shakespearean criticism does not necessarily constitute a proportionate reflection of movements derived from, or even crucially important to, modern thought in general. In other words, some influential thinkers simply have not written on Shakespeare, or even on literature. Also, a given school of criticism may affect some one sector of Shakespeare studies while leaving others untouched. Structuralism, for example, which uses methods of structural linguistics and structural anthropology, has had, in Dubrow's opinion, only a slight influence on criticism of the plays, although "it had a marked effect on approaches to Shakespeare's non-dramatic poetry." Similarly, the deconstructionist theories prevalent in the 1980s "enjoyed only a brief and limited impact on Shakespeare studies."[2]

This chapter will deal with critical works that are concerned primarily with *Julius Caesar*. As a result, some famous names in contemporary Shakespearean criticism may turn up missing. Not everyone has gotten around to writing about every play. Some of the works described here are short and self-sufficient essays, others are larger works that discuss *Julius Caesar* as the main subject or a substantial part of the main subject. I have tried to give a sufficiently detailed description for the author's method to become apparent.

ARCHETYPAL AND PSYCHOANALYTICAL CRITICISM

Both Jung and Freud dealt with the human unconscious. Jung hypothesized that each individual's mind contains, already installed in a sense, an inherited "collective unconscious," a racial memory formed by the repeated experiences of our ancestors. This collective unconscious is filled with "primordial images," or archetypes. Freud also postulated an unconscious part of the mind but focused on the individual's personal history for its contents, suggesting that an individual's painful memories were suppressed and sent into storage, so to speak, in the unconscious, where they are ordinarily inaccessible to the conscious mind.

In Shakespearean literary criticism, these two approaches merge to some extent, since each helps to account for the appeal that literary patterns have always had for human beings. We respond to these patterns because they are aligned to the contents of our unconscious minds, whether these contents have been inherited from our ancestors, as in Jung's view, or derived from our personal (but suppressed and thus forgotten) experiences, as in Freud's. Thus, an emphasis on myth and ritual is typical of both Jungian (archetypal) and Freudian (psychoanalytical) literary criticism. Myths tell universal stories that resonate in our subconscious minds for reasons unknown to our rational selves. Rituals let us perform symbolic actions that are also connected to these secret patterns.

Freud, according to Norman Holland, mentions *Julius Caesar* only in passing.[3] Otto Rank, a student of Freud, wrote a more extended analysis of *Julius Caesar* in 1912, emphasizing the idea of father-son conflict. Rank sees Brutus as a son figure whose feelings for the father figure Julius Caesar are ambiguously mixed of love and hatred. Cassius and Antony are also son figures; Cassius embodies a self-punishing urge, while Antony represents filial piety. The conspirators' defeat is caused by their unconscious remorse.[4]

Ernest Jones, writing in the first half of the twentieth century, applies Freudian analytical techniques to *Hamlet* and mentions *Julius Caesar* when discussing the connection between fathers and kings. "Psychoanalytical work has shown," Jones observes, "that a ruler . . . is in the unconscious mind a typical father symbol, and in actual life he tends to draw on to himself the ambivalent attitude characteristic of the son's feeling for the father. . . . Very little experience of life is enough to show that the popular feelings about any ruler are always disproportionate, whether they are positive or negative."[5] Jones also points out "the psychological origin of revolutionary tendencies in the primordial rebellion against the father."[6]

In the late 1950s, Gordon Ross Smith viewed Brutus in the light of "a tyrannical superego in its struggle against both id and ego."[7] Noting that Freud had seen the superego as "popularly equated with conscience," the id as the "unconscious and often anti-social forces in mental life," and the ego as "the function of mediation between the individual and external reality," Smith classes Brutus with "impractical and ineffectual reformers, do-gooders, and like persons." Such a person, Smith says, "(1) will be highly idealistic, (2) will be very conscious of his own moral superiority, (3) will think he is best fitted to direct affairs, (4) will make incessant mistakes in his evaluations of reality, (5) will ignore or defy these errors . . . (6) will employ rationalization. . . . Clearly this little constellation of patterns is the essence of Brutus's character."[8]

By 1964, Norman Holland's *Psychoanalysis and Shakespeare*, cited in connection with Freud and Rank, was able to demonstrate by its bulk that the psychoanalytical approach had borne considerable fruit when applied to Shakespeare. Holland's thorough and useful book offers both a general survey and a commentary on individual works.[9]

Edward T. Herbert has combined archetypal and Freudian terminology, observing that "the plot is a dramatization of an archetypal situation such as that discussed by Freud in *Totem and Taboo*. Speculating on the origins of religion, Freud reconstructs the conditions of the primal horde and discusses the attitude toward the ruler. He finds a strain of mistrust pervading the members of the clan toward their ruler, whom they worship as a god one day and slay as a criminal the next."[10] Herbert emphasizes Caesar's role as father, pointing out that Cassius compares himself and Caesar to a mythological father and son in his anecdote of his and Caesar's swimming competition:

> I, as Aeneas, our great ancestor,
> Did from the flames of Troy upon his shoulder
> The old Anchises bear, so from the waves of Tiber
> Did I the tired Caesar.   (I.ii.112–115)

Herbert points out that "in order for Caesar to play the role of a father, it is essential that all the conspirators be portrayed as young men.[11] Shakespeare emphasizes this quality of youthfulness, according to Herbert, when the conspirators, wondering whether to include Cicero, mention Cicero's "silver hairs" in contrast to their own "youths and wildness" (II.i.144, 148).

Lynn de Gerenday also sees Brutus as filled with inner contradictions, attempting, for example, in the quarrel scene of IV.iii, to "resist any ambivalent interpretations of Caesar's murder by excessive condemnation of Cassius."[12] War, for Brutus, "is a ritualization of his need to be defeated and punished, his need to fail as a reparation for his aggression against Caesar."

René Girard discusses *Julius Caesar* with regard to the function of sacrifice in primitive ritual.[13] Girard points out that Brutus refers to his ancestor, an earlier Brutus dating from the legendary history of Rome, who had led the expulsion of the last king and thus helped found the Roman Republic to which Brutus is idealistically bound:

> My ancestors did from the streets of Rome
> The Tarquin drive, when he was call'd a king.   (II.i.53–54)

This, Girard claims, is the standard justification for sacrifice: "They [sacrificers] must do again what their ancestors did when the community was founded."[14] Brutus then strives to make sure the death of Caesar will be perceived as a necessary ritual, undertaken for the good of the community. His refusal to kill Mark Antony is part of this effort, as are several of his other suggestions:

> Let's be sacrificers but not butchers, Caius . . .
> Let's kill him boldly but not wrathfully;
> Let's carve him as a dish fit for the gods.   (II.i.166, 172–173)

Citing the Indian Brahmanas on the function of sacrifice as "the originator and rejuvenation of culture,"[15] Girard goes on to point out that Brutus is unable to follow through on his intentions. The Roman mob, thanks in large part to Antony, does not accept the assassination of Caesar as a necessary sacrifice. Brutus then ironically becomes, in effect, a sacrificial victim himself. His suicide, "preceded by an invocation of Caesar, is interpreted as the first sacrifice of the new cult. This sacrificial meaning is the one that Mark Antony and Octavius embrace in their funeral eulogies. Octavius is the first Roman emperor, so it is appropriate that he should play the role of high priest."[16]

FEMINIST CRITICISM

Feminist criticism is in a sense the other side of the coin from psychoanalytical criticism. Feminists generally take the view that Freud and his followers see the world in a masculinized, patriarchal, and, consequently, distorted light. In setting out to redress the balance, feminist Shakespearean critics tend to gravitate toward the strong female characters. *Julius Caesar* has received comparatively little attention, having only two female characters, both marginal to the action. What critical work does exist, however, serves to examplify a number of feminist concerns.

Gail Kern Paster suggests that the murder of Caesar represents a symbolic attempt by the conspirators to transform him into a woman and thus to free themselves from the threat represented by Caesar's live, unbleeding, masculine self.[17] Women, Paster explains, were perceived in Shakespeare's time as weak creatures, menstruating in a seeping sort of way and passively unable to stop bleeding. Women's menstrual blood was seen as involuntary; Caesar's bleeding body, powerless in death, partakes of this womanly, involuntary, and silent helplessness. The conspirators do not enjoy their victory for long, however. Their transformation of Caesar into a woman soon turns against them. Caesar's rescuer arrives in the person of Mark Antony, who, Paster observes, uses "Petrarchan vocabulary"—the language of Renaissance love poetry—when he emphasizes the "female vulnerability" of Caesar's mantle, unable to resist the daggers of his killers. The mob's sympathy then swings to Caesar, presented in the role of a helpless and violated female.

Barbara L. Parker draws parallels between prostitution, Catholicism, and the assassination of Caesar, as Shakespeare's audience would presumably have seen these parallels.[18] Parker's article is not aligned with strictly feminist concerns at every point but does emphasize images of the body, particularly male-female and sexual images, and focuses on gender reversals. Pointing out a startling number of sexual puns—a pun in almost every line it would seem—Parker sees the play as a burlesque of Catholic rituals and imagery.[19] Calphurnia's dream of Caesar's statue spouting blood becomes a "grotesque parody of the redeeming Christ," an image derived from the medieval emblem of the Christ-like mother pelican, who, according to folklore, pecks her own breast to feed her young with her own blood.[20] An illicit religion (Catholicism, as seen by Shakespeare's audience) is also paralleled by illicit sexuality. Parker sees the Forum scene as "the play's sexual climax and one of the most ingenious seduction scenes in literature."[21] Antony orchestrates the crowd's coitus with the corpse of Caesar. His speech "waxes progressively more erotic; eventually he transmutes the corpse itself into a phallus and the crowd into the receiving agent":

> You will compel me then to read the will?
> Then make a ring about the corpse of Caesar.   (III.ii.159–160)

The crowd's eventual outburst of rage becomes in this analogy an orgasm, with fiery accompaniment, as the crowd sets out to burn Caesar's body and the conspirators' houses. These flames are "emblematic of sexual frenzy" and "mark the play's structural climax as well. Thereafter, the fire imagery all but vanishes, reflecting the detumescence characterizing the second half of the play."[22]

A feminist perspective on Calphurnia and Portia is offered by Madelon Sprengnether, who emphasizes the "anxiety concerning femininity" in *Julius Caesar*.[23] "Caesar's death results, in an immediate sense, from his fear of appearing foolish or womanly by attending seriously to Calphurnia's dream," while Portia "articulates the fundamental masculine ethic of the play by voluntarily wounding herself to demonstrate her capacity for Stoic endurance and to win her husband's confidence. . . . In her zeal to prove her masculine trustworthiness, she reveals the underlying paradox of the play, which equates manliness with injury, so that the sign of masculinity becomes the wound."

Cynthia Marshall combines linguistics and feminist approaches; she is concerned with the verbal powerlessness of *Julius Caesar*'s two female characters.[24] Portia's two acts of violence, both directed against herself—cutting her own thigh and swallowing fire—suggest that she "is in revolt against the symbolic order, against language as a structure of power."[25] Left out of the masculine conversation, allowed no part in the conspiracy aside from her own determination to find out what her husband is doing, Portia displays her "ability to perform by Stoic standards" and "momentarily destabilizes the masculine code by claiming it as her own."[26] Calphurnia, similarly left out of things, does not even get to describe her own dream (II.ii.76–79), which is "narrated by the appropriating Caesar"; this takeover "demonstrates an effacement of her linguistic presence."[27] Decius Brutus, by supplying a false interpretation of Calphurnia's dream, continues the process of taking it away from her. Yet Calphurnia retains a kind of power. Her dream "offers a model of intuitive understanding"; in it, Caesar's statue runs with blood, and Caesar himself will soon follow suit. Calphurnia has thus been "given an independence from the linguistic order"; she and her dream are "validated in the play by the realization of her prophecy."[28]

Coppélia Kahn's 1997 book on the Roman plays offers detailed studies of Shakespeare's narrative poem "The Rape of Lucrece," as well as of the Roman plays: *Titus Andronicus, Julius Caesar, Antony and Cleopatra, Coriolanus*, and *Cymbeline*. Seeing "the image of the wound as a fetish of Roman masculinity,"[29] Kahn examines the view, found in Aristotle and Machiavelli, that "the republic is a distinctly masculine sphere in which debate and action, the exercise of reason and freedom, make men truly virile."[30] A feminist element does enter the world of politics in the guise of Fortune, "the traditionally feminized realm of mutability and insecurity"; thus the revenge that Antony evokes for Caesar's death "has a feminine character. . . . Unrestrained emotions deaf to the general good and inaccessible to reason overtake the Roman Republic and its new leaders."[31] Brutus becomes "a tragic hero who, though he entertains moral strictures against killing that are associated with the feminine and the private, must embrace a man's duty and repress them in the name of defending an abstract concept of the public weal." In Brutus, then, "the contradictions embedded in his culture are set at war."[32]

SEMIOTICS

Semiotics, the study of the nature of signs, according to Terence Hawkes, seeks to discover "how meaning is produced in society, and thus concerns itself with the whole range of the process of signification and communication."[33] This seems a far-ranging aspiration, perhaps not immediately adjacent to our concerns in this chapter. However, the study of semiotics has been applied by Alessandro Serpieri in increasing concentration of focus to literature, to drama, to Shakespeare, and finally to *Julius Caesar.*

In *Julius Caesar*, according to Serpieri, Shakespeare presents two models of the world: the "symbolic model," described as "a classical-medieval-Renaissance heritage," and the "syntagmatic model," which inaugurates "the relativism of the modern age." These two models, Serpieri finds, reflect "two distinct visions of language itself as the primary modeling system of a culture: *motivated* language versus *arbitrary* language."[34]

Caesar and Antony, members of the symbolic world order, represent "the motivated name"; their opponents, Brutus and Cassius, derive from the syntagmatic world order and represent "the arbitrary name." Serpieri discusses a key passage in which, "during his political seduction of Brutus, Cassius attacks, among other things, the very heart of the symbolic world-order, i.e. the motivated Name":

> Brutus and Caesar: what should be in that "Caesar"?
> Why should that name be sounded more than yours?
> Write them together, yours is as fair a name;
> Sound them, it doth become the mouth as well. (I.ii.140–143)

Names, then, to the syntagmatic world order, are relative. To the symbolic world order, names are absolute. "By contrast, Caesar identifies himself completely with his name. His ideological self-deception lies in his living and dying for that name, which he hammers out continually by speaking of himself in the third person."

Since Caesar, along with his name, remains powerful even after death, and the syntagmatic conspirators commit suicide, it might seem that Serpieri is suggesting a victory for the symbolic world model. However, Serpieri claims that this is not the case. Shakespearean drama

> encodes the crumbling of the symbolic model, with its centripetal ideology and its stabilizing rhetoric, but rarely permits a positive perception of the syntagmatic model that erodes it through its centrifugal ideology and its destabi-

lizing rhetoric. . . . In dramatizing history as a clash of models, [Shakespeare] is careful not to declare allegiance to one side or the other, thereby transmitting a message. He limits himself, rather, to an attentive comparison of the ideologies in question, anchoring them to discourse and to the speaking subjects, and always revealing in them components of partiality and blindness.

NEW HISTORICISM

The new historical critical approach is to some extent related to traditional historical studies. In both, a literary text is considered in relation to the world in which the text was created and in which it found its original audience. In the case of a literary work set in a period different from that of its original audience, both traditional and new historians are frequently concerned with what the original audience knew about this earlier period and how they might have felt about it.

A major difference between traditional and new historicism involves angle of view. Traditionally historians have dealt with highly visible events—wars and treaties, kings and courts, diplomats and summit meetings. New historicists, by contrast, have emphasized the lives of the unempowered, the common people, often seeing these as exploited victims of the ruling classes.

The term "new historicism" presents some difficulties in labeling. Other variously named critical movements are related to new historicism and may overlap it. Cultural materialism, for example, has been described as the British version of new historicism, though with some differences, among them a more strenuous emphasis on Marxism.[35]

With regard to literature, new historicists tend to feel that the values intrinsic to the literature produced by, or at any rate approved and tolerated by, the ruling classes are implicitly a manufactured product, intended to keep the lower classes from rebelling. Thus, for example, a reader's perception that Renaissance literature often presents a pattern of universal harmony, hierarchically organized of contented components that have no desire to depart from their appointed places, would become from a new historicist's standpoint highly suspicious. E.M.W. Tillyard's *The Elizabethan World Picture* (1943) and the same author's *Shakespeare's History Plays* (1944) have been frequent new historicist targets. Alexander Leggatt, however, may have indicated a reverse swing of the pendulum by declining to go in for Tillyard bashing:

> We have established that to see Shakespeare as a propagandist for the Tudor Myth, the Great Chain of Being, and the Elizabethan World Picture will not do. So far so good. But in fairness to Tillyard it should be said that his book contains much that is wise and sensitive. . . . There is a current tendency to see society as a structure of oppression and exploitation, and to read Shakespeare accordingly. We will get at part of the truth in that way, but only part.[36]

As Leggatt implies, new historicists often see Shakespeare in one of two possible roles. He may have been merely a limb of the establishment, dramatizing the official party line. A second option is to view Shakespeare as a secret subversive, encoding in his plays messages of encouragement to the downtrodden.

It follows that new historicists frequently deal with the idea of theatrical representation in itself. The fact that monarchs and other powerful figures can be exhibited on a stage, acted by common players, creates a subversive situation, subtly undermining the hierarchy of the state and thus annoying to the authorities. The Elizabethan and Jacobean insistence on the licensing of plays through the office of the Master of the Revels supports this assumption. Theatrical companies were required to submit new scripts to be examined for seditious or irreligious material.[37]

The idea of the theater as a subversive enterprise leads us to a real-life figure much discussed among new historicists, a figure who can be associated with *Julius Caesar*, albeit somewhat tangentially. Robert Devereux, second earl of Essex (1566–1601), was one of Queen Elizabeth's favorites, renowned for his military victories in Ireland. In 1601, Essex turned against his sovereign, attempted unsuccessfully to raise a rebellion against her, and was executed. The direct Shakespearean connection here is with the play *Richard II*, a special performance of which was arranged by some of Essex's supporters shortly before the uprising. Since the action of *Richard II* turns on the deposition of a monarch, Shakespeare's company was briefly under suspicion of complicity in the plot.

Essex's rebellion and fall occurred after *Julius Caesar* was written, so he could hardly have been a model for Brutus, the role to which he seems retrospectively best fitted. However, Wayne A. Rebhorn draws a parallel between Essex and Caesar.[38] At the beginning of the play, Caesar has returned in triumph from a military expedition, a circumstance that aligns him with Essex at that point in Essex's career. In *Henry V*, written in the same year as *Julius Caesar*, 1599, Shakespeare not only makes a specific reference to Essex but links him with Caesar. The Chorus is describing King Henry's arrival in London after the victory of Agincourt:

> How London doth pour out her citizens!
> The Mayor and all his brethren in best sort,
> Like to the senators of th'antique Rome,
> With the Plebians swarming at their heels,
> Go forth and fetch their conqu'ring Caesar in.   (*Henry V*, V. Prologue.24–28)

The Chorus then invites the earl of Essex into the picture:

> As by a lower but by loving likelihood,
> Were now the general of our gracious Empress,
> As in good time he may, from Ireland coming,
> Bringing rebellion broached on his sword,
> How many would the peaceful city quit
> To welcome him!   (25–34)

There has been some doubt that these last lines actually refer to the earl of Essex,[39] but most scholars seem to accept the identification. Rebhorn observes, "If Shakespeare thinks of Essex as Julius Caesar in *Henry V*, is it not most likely he was thinking about him as well in *Julius Caesar*?"[40]

Jonathan Goldberg finds another connection between an English monarch and Shakespeare's *Julius Caesar*. Goldberg analyzes the writings of James I, who succeeded Queen Elizabeth and reigned from 1603 until his death in 1625. King James betook himself to print fairly often for a busy monarch, expressing his opinions of witchcraft and tobacco among other matters, but the piece with which Goldberg is most concerned is the *Basilikon Doran*, the king's statement on kingship. Here King James declared himself a king by divine right, ruling "in the style of the gods."[41]

These gods, Goldberg suggests, were Roman gods. King James based his idea of political authority on the Roman model, favoring, for example, the Palladian (neoclassical) architecture of Inigo Jones. "Jones's architectural fantasies, spun out in the décor of Jacobean and Caroline masques, express imagined power, just as the Banqueting House at Whitehall, which he [Jones] designed, served as the place where masques were performed and where ambassadors and royal guests met and were received."[42] *Julius Caesar*, although not a masque, nevertheless portrayed Roman power in a positive light, and according to Goldberg the king saw himself as an actor playing a Caesar-like role, "constant, unchanging, unique—a single star, unmoving."[43] The fact that Shakespeare wrote *Julius Caesar* several years before James I began his reign does not, according to Goldberg, affect this association. Presumably if James I had disapproved of *Julius Caesar*, he would not have allowed it to be acted.

John Drakakis, in a discussion of *Julius Caesar*, exemplifies the interest taken by new historicists in the subtleties of theatrical reality. Drakakis points out that Cassius and Casca "fashion" Brutus as if they were preparing an actor for a role (I.ii); Brutus, in turn, "grasps the importance of mediating the conspiracy through existing rituals and institutions," including those related to the theater. "In a culture in which those who would oppose theatrical representation continued to insist upon the power that adheres in the theatrical image itself, *Julius Caesar* is not so much a celebration of theater as an unmasking of the politics of representation per se."[44]

Richard A. Burt is largely concerned with theoretical issues as he investigates the meaning of political criticism, but in the process he touches specifically on *Julius Caesar*. Burt's analysis of the play's class structure can be seen as forming a link with today's social issues:

> Brutus speaks as if the general good and the patricians' interests were the same: all are Romans. Yet inscribed within the general good is a class division between patrician and plebe. It is the patricians, not the plebes, who fear being put in awe of one man, and it is the patricians who believe that they will save Rome. . . . Antony's populist rhetoric in the Forum succeeds partly because Brutus has already positioned the plebians as subjects rather than as citizens, as the recipients of their freedom from above. . . . When Antony overturns Brutus's construction of Caesar as an ambitious tyrant, all of Antony's examples are related to the way Caesar served the plebians' interests. . . . Thus the

conspirators become traitors for having murdered the man most able to benefit Rome.[45]

Richard Wilson has written an extended study of the play from the new historicist perspective. Wilson sees *Julius Caesar* as embodying social and political concerns that were to become more visible in the decades following the play's initial
production in 1599. Shakespeare's play becomes "a dress rehearsal for England's
seventeenth-century revolution . . . it relates the struggle for power in Shakespearean Rome to the contest between competing ideologies in Elizabethan and
Jacobean politics." A clue to this contemporary frame of reference exists within
the play itself: "Critics are embarrassed that Shakespeare's Romans wear feather
hats and hear chiming clocks; the coincidence between the stage and the actual
state implies that these anachronisms were not unconscious."[46]

Wilson gives considerable emphasis to the play's opening scene. Here the
Roman workingmen, the cobblers and carpenters, walk the streets instead of tend-
ing to their trades, and walk, moreover, without wearing or carrying any emblem
of their social identity. Wilson makes a connection here with Elizabethan politics,
in which established power seems always to have run scared, citing a 1563 Statute
of Artificers stipulating "fines for workers who left their workplace or failed to
signal their identity in their mechanics' outfits." Such anonymity was perceived by
the authorities as threatening to the established hierarchy. "What makes these arti-
sans so menacing is not that they flaunt the craftsman's clogs and leather apron,
but that without them they are unreadable. In their Sunday 'best apparel' . . . they
can even be mistaken for their betters."[47]

HOMOSEXUAL CRITICISM

Some awkwardness in terminology occurs here, in that neither of the critical
works mentioned in this section has been labeled homosexual by its respective author. Appropriate critical terminology does not seem quite to have jelled. Dubrow
has suggested the categories "Gay and Lesbian Criticism" or "Queer Theory."[48] I
have chosen the wording of the heading for convenience.

Bruce R. Smith, though he uses the word "homosexual" in his title, sees himself
as actually a new historicist. "The study I have undertaken here is 'historicist' because, unlike formalist New Criticism in the 1930s or Deconstructionism in the
1970s, it insists on putting literary texts in historical context, 'new' because it asks
questions that seem vital to us in our own moment in history."[49] Smith does not
focus in detail on *Julius Caesar*, but he does discuss the popularity in Shakespeare's time of Plutarch's *Lives of the Noble Grecians and Romans*:

> The all-male power structure of sixteenth- and seventeenth-century society
> fostered male bonds above all other emotional ties. . . . For most sixteenth-
> century readers the very act of reading North's translation of Plutarch was an
> exercise in homosociality. . . . As a sourcebook on what it meant to be male in

classical antiquity, Plutarch . . . offered Renaissance readers a model of male
bonding that closely matched the ways in which men related to men in their
own society. . . . Plutarch's heroes move in a world defined totally in terms of
political bonds. In this intensely masculine world emotional ties are a function
of political ties.[50]

G. Wilson Knight, writing in the early 1930s before the flowering of many of
today's critical complexities, sees the characters' various loves as "emotional, fiery,
but not exactly sexual, not physically passionate; even Portia and Brutus love with a
gentle companionship rather than any passion."[51] Antony's love for Caesar, as Knight
sees it, is simpler and thus stronger than Brutus's more complex love for Caesar:
"Brutus loves him [Caesar] as a man but believes in him only too powerfully as a
hero, and thinks him therefore dangerous. To Antony, the two aspects are indistin-
guishable."[52] Cassius too enjoys a stronger love than Brutus can manage. In the quarrel scene between Brutus and Cassius (IV.iii), "Cassius is always in touch with
realities—of love, of conspiracy, of war: Brutus is ever most at home with his ethical abstractions."[53] Brutus's tragedy, in short, is his inability to love, although he
comes closest to affection for his young servant Lucius, "his truest love."[54]

NOTES

1. Terence Hawkes, "Shakespeare and the New Critical Approaches," in Stanley Wells,
ed., *The Cambridge Companion to Shakespeare Studies* (Cambridge: Cambridge University Press, 1986), pp. 287–302. Jonathan Dollimore, "Critical Developments: Cultural Materialism, Feminism and Gender Critique, and New Historicism," in Stanley Wells, ed.,
Shakespeare: A Bibliographical Guide (Oxford: Clarendon Press, 1990), pp. 405–428.

2. Heather Dubrow, *Riverside Shakespeare*, 2d ed. (Boston: Houghton, 1997), p. 40.

3. It seems that Freud once dreamed that he played the part of Brutus. Norman Holland,
Psychoanalysis and Shakespeare (New York: McGraw-Hill, 1964; repr. Octagon Books,
1976), p. 64. For this detail, Holland cites Freud's "Dostoevsky and Parricide" (1928).
Freud's most extensive Shakepearean commentary is made on *Hamlet*, although Holland
points out (p. 63) that he sometimes misquoted the text.

4. Holland, in ibid. (p. 212), discusses these ideas from Rank's *Das Inzest-Motiv in
Dichtung und Sage* (1912).

5. Ernest Jones, *Hamlet and Oedipus* (New York: Doubleday, 1949; repr. Norton,
1976), pp. 121–122. Jones developed this book from several essays on the same general
ideas, the first published in 1910.

6. Ibid., p. 122.

7. Gordon Ross Smith, "Brutus, Virtue, and Will," *SQ* 10 (1959), 379.

8. Ibid.

9. Among the works Holland mentions under *Julius Caesar* (pp. 212–214) are Samuel
A. Tannenbaum, "Psychoanalytical Gleanings from Shakespeare," *Psyche and Eros* 1
(1920), 29–39, and Harold Feldman, "Unconscious Envy in Brutus," *AI* 9 (1959), 307–335.

10. Edward T. Herbert, "Myth and Archetype in *Julius Caesar*," *Psychoanalytical Review* 57 (1970), 303. Herbert also mentions James Frazier's *The Golden Bough* (1890),
which deals extensively with primitive tribes and their kings, and which influenced Freud.

11. Ibid., p. 307.

12. Lynn de Gerenday, "Play, Ritualization, and Ambivalence in *Julius Caesar*," *L&P* 24 (1974), 31.

13. René Girard, *A Theatre of Envy: William Shakespeare* (New York: Oxford University Press, 1991), pp. 185–226. Girard's emphasis on group rather than private rituals would seem to put him into the archetypal camp, but he employs Freudian ideas as well.

14. Ibid., p. 210.

15. Ibid., p. 213.

16. Ibid., p. 221.

17. Gail Kern Paster, " 'In the Spirit of Men There Is No Blood': Blood as Trope of Gender in *Julius Caesar*," *SQ* 40 (1989), 284–298.

18. Barbara L. Parker, "The Whore of Babylon and Shakespeare's *Julius Caesar*," *SEL* 35 (1995), 251–269.

19. Parker's interpretations are aided by Frankie Rubenstein's *A Dictionary of Shakespeare's Sexual Puns and Their Significance* (London: Macmillan, 1984); Eric Partridge's *Shakespeare's Bawdy* (London: Routledge, 1947, 1968); and the *Oxford English Dictionary*.

20. Ibid., p. 254.

21. Ibid., p. 256.

22. Ibid.

23. Madelon Sprengnether, "Annihilating Intimacy in *Coriolanus*," in Mary Beth Rose, ed., *Women in the Middle Ages and the Renaissance: Literary and Historical Perspectives* (Syracuse, N.Y.: Syracuse University Press, 1986), p. 96.

24. Cynthia Marshall, "Portia's Wound, Calphurnia's Dream," *ELR* 24 (1994), 471–488.

25. Ibid., p. 478.

26. Ibid., p. 476.

27. Ibid., p. 483.

28. Ibid., p. 487.

29. Coppélia Kahn, *Roman Shakespeare: Warriors, Wounds, and Women* (London: Routledge, 1997), p. iii.

30. Ibid., p. 83.

31. Ibid., pp. 84, 104–105.

32. Ibid., pp. 99, 105.

33. Hawkes, "Shakespeare," p. 293.

34. Alessandro Serpieri, "Reading the Signs: Towards a Semiotics of Shakespearean Drama," trans. Keir Elam, in John Drakakis, ed., *Alternative Shakespeares* (London: Methuen, 1985), pp. 119–143. This and the following quotations are from pp. 125–127.

35. Michael Cohen's brief but highly readable "New Directions in Shakespeare Criticism," *ShN* 38 (Fall–Winter 1988), 38–39, makes this distinction.

36. Alexander Leggatt, *Shakespeare's Political Drama: The History Plays and the Roman Plays* (London: Routledge, 1988), p. x.

37. See "The Theatre and the Authorities," in Russ McDonald, *The Bedford Companion to Shakespeare: An Introduction with Documents* (Boston: Bedford Books of St. Martin's Press, 1996), pp. 54–57.

38. Wayne A. Rebhorn, "The Crisis of the Aristocracy in *Julius Caesar*," *RenQ* 43 (1990), 75–111.

39. Warren D. Smith suggests that these lines were written by another hand for a later court performance and that "the general of our gracious Empress" was in fact Charles

Blount, who also achieved victories in Ireland. "The *Henry V* Choruses in the First Folio," *JEGP* 53 (1954), 38–57.

40. Rebhorn, "Crisis," p. 100.

41. Jonathan Goldberg, *James I and the Politics of Literature: Jonson, Shakespeare, Donne, and Their Contemporaries* (Baltimore: Johns Hopkins University Press, 1983), p. xi.

42. Ibid., p. 39.

43. Ibid., p. 166.

44. John Drakakis, "Fashion It Thus: *Julius Caesar* and the Politics of Theatrical Representation," *ShS* 44 (1992), 71–72.

45. Richard A. Burt, " 'A Dangerous Rome': Shakespeare's *Julius Caesar* and the Discursive Determinism of Cultural Politics," in Marie-Rose Logan and Peter L. Rudnytsky, eds., *Contending Kingdoms: Historical, Psychological, and Feminist Approaches to the Literature of Sixteenth-Century England and France* (Detroit, Mich.: Wayne State University Press, 1991), pp. 120–121.

46. Richard Wilson, *Julius Caesar* (London: Penguin, 1992), pp. 1–2.

47. Ibid., pp. 23–24.

48. Dubrow, *Riverside Shakespeare*, p. 44.

49. Bruce R. Smith, *Homosexual Desire in Shakespeare's England: A Cultural Poetics* (Chicago: University of Chicago Press, 1991), p. 277, n. 45.

50. Ibid., pp. 56, 57.

51. G. Wilson Knight, *The Imperial Theme: Further Interpretations of Shakespeare's Tragedies Including the Roman Plays* (London: Oxford University Press, 1931, 1939), p. 63.

52. Ibid., pp. 66–67.

53. Ibid., p. 75.

54. Ibid., p. 81.

6

THE PLAY IN PERFORMANCE

A shift from simple to elaborate production, then back again to simplicity, sums up much of *Julius Caesar*'s stage history for the past four hundred years, as it does the stage history of Shakespeare's plays in general. Which model, then, should be adopted as the best way to realize Shakespeare? Actor-managers of the eighteenth and nineteenth centuries, delighting in every special effect their scenic designers could contrive and their carpenters put together, might have claimed that Shakespeare made full use of the theatrical facilities at his disposal and would have used more had he had them. Reformers of more recent times might reply that a bare stage allows an audience to use its imagination, to reconstitute mentally the world Shakespeare has blueprinted in his dialogue.

Both sides of the debate make telling points. It is true that the grand and cumbersome scenery of olden days, along with the curtain lowering required when the grand and cumbersome scenery had to be changed to make way for the next scene, stopped the flow of the action. It may also have competed with the actors. An audience enchanted by, say, a perspective vista of the Roman Forum may not have paid strict attention to the dialogue, even if the dialogue were then considering some necessary question of the play. Nevertheless, the theater managers were following principles they genuinely felt to be appropriate. Visual splendor was meant to enhance Shakespeare's meaning, not to distract from it. Often, in fact, the lavish settings were based on historical research, or what managers and audiences accepted as historical research if one factors in the appeal of the picturesque, and thus could claim to have added dimensions of authenticity.

The bare platform stage, on the other hand, whatever its theoretical superiority for the improvement of the audience's imagination, has an undeniable potential for boredom. The upshot is that Shakespearean productions today often borrow from both schools of thought, taking what directors consider the best from each. The twentieth-century ideal of continuously flowing action is kept, but the stage is often allowed embellishments by way not only of acting areas on various levels,

The Elizabethan stage relied on the audience's imagination rather than on illusionist scenery. Sketch by Jo McMurtry, 1997, based in part on the reconstructed Shakespeare's Globe in London.

which were present in Shakespeare's day, but of large architectural constructions, brought in on a revolve or lowered from the flies without slowing the pace.

In film, the twentieth century's great contribution to art, action can be continuous no matter how complicated the setting. Perhaps for this reason, there does not seem to be a great deal of brow furrowing among practitioners of this medium on whether to provide an illusion of reality. Films just do it. In general, they go in for as much visual appeal, even spectacle, as the budget will allow.

While the question of elaborate versus simple staging applies to Shakespeare's plays as a whole, *Julius Caesar* has its own aspects to be considered in planning a production or, from the audience's standpoint, in analyzing a performance one has just seen. To what extent, for example, does this play's political content, with its examination of such questions as tyranny and assassination, connect with the audience's own world? Are the characters to be interpreted in a hero-and-villain pattern, or as more of a mixture? Is the text to be cut, and if so, on what principles?

With regard to political parallels, the audience's relationship to the world of the play has naturally varied according to the audience's own time and place. Tyrants come and go in history, while assassinations are unfortunately so frequent that a new one may crowd out, at least for a time, the public memory of its predecessors. These historical links are sometimes subtly implied; in other productions, they are emphasized until they may seem to have usurped the whole purpose of the play.

With regard to its characters, *Julius Caesar* presents a special problem or, perhaps, a special opportunity. The roles of Brutus, Cassius, and Antony require actors who can rise above the level of mere competence; that of Julius Caesar requires at least an actor of authority and presence. Casting can thus be hard on the budget. It might also be hard on a leading actor's ego. Both David Garrick, in the eighteenth century, and Henry Irving, in the nineteenth, were ardent Shakespeareans but showed no interest in presenting *Julius Caesar*, and it is possible that each preferred to dominate his own stage with no rivals in the immediate vicinity. On the other hand, for a director who has several strong actors available, *Julius Caesar* would be a natural choice.

Even if a spirit of equality prevails among the actors undertaking *Julius Caesar*, questions of interpretation remain. Is Brutus to be acted as a noble idealist, tempted into assassination by the strength of his principles—one who does the wrong deed, but for the right reason? Or is he a self-deceived figurehead, led around by the other conspirators? Is Cassius a cold manipulator or an emotional firebrand? Is Julius Caesar the embryonic tyrant Brutus thinks he is, arrogant and unfeeling, or simply a human being who behaves in an authoritative manner in order to lead his country effectively? Is Mark Antony a loyal friend, true blue, revenging Caesar's death with all the passion he claims to have, or a shrewd opportunist who knows a power vacuum when he sees one?

Once a character's interpretation has been clarified for a production, textual cuts may be useful in solidifying the choice. If Brutus is to be seen as a nondupe, for example, Cassius may lose the lines in which he describes planting forged letters where Brutus can find them (I.ii.315–330; iii.142–146); this action highlights Cassius's manipulative shrewdness, but at the expense of Brutus. A straightforward and sincere Brutus generally hears of Portia's death only once (IV.iii.147–158, 181–193), and a resolute Brutus is allowed to commit suicide without previously telling Cassius he would never do such a thing (V.i.103–107). Similarly, an arrogantly superhuman Julius Caesar, approaching the tyrannical, often does not admit such a human failing as deafness (I.ii.213–214).

Mark Antony's interpretation has perhaps the simplest textual pointer. When in Shakespeare's text he appears among the new rulers of Rome, calmly deciding which enemies will or will not be executed (IV.i, known as the proscription scene), his character as noble avenger, seemingly so strongly defined in the Forum scene when he wins over the plebeians to Caesar's cause, goes pretty much out the window. Cutting this scene will naturally bolster the more heroic view of Antony. Leaving it in, as present-day productions tend to do, gives the audience a gloomy though familiar feeling of disillusionment with knights in shining armor, wherever encountered.

For a stage production to make textual cuts at all is in violation of the purest tenets of early twentieth-century Shakespearean reform. Reformers have assumed that Shakespeare's actors worked from a full text, else Shakespeare would not have written the full text, and that modern productions should follow suit in order to do justice to the plays. This advice is more easily given than followed. In *Julius Caesar*, cuts are used not only to reinforce character interpretation, but also to make the action more coherent, from the standpoint of an audience not familiar with the play or the history behind it. Cuts also serve to reduce playing time, often an essential consideration.

In order to streamline the plot, minor characters have sometimes been removed altogether or combined with other characters. Murellus and Flavius, for example, the tribunes who reprimand the people in the opening scene and do not reappear in the play, are occasionally replaced by two of the anti-Caesar senators whom the audience will later get to know. Casca, Trebonius, and Metellus have done duty here. Again, while Shakespeare's text brings in a group of completely new minor characters for Acts IV and V, a favorite alteration has been to include with these a few of the more familiar conspirators from the first three acts, giving them lines the text has assigned to the confusing newcomers and thus, presumably, strengthening the continuity between the two parts of the play.

In this way one sometimes finds that two minor characters have been rolled into one. The Soothsayer, who warns Caesar to beware the Ides of March (I.ii.18, 23), is rather frequently merged with Artemidorus, who tries to give Caesar a list of the conspirators planning to kill him (II.iii; III.i.3). Other minor characters disappear altogether. A frequent casualty is the "camp poet" who visits Brutus and Cassius at Sardis (IV.iii.124–138).

A minor character who does not advance the action, but whose significance is increasingly recognized nevertheless, is another poet, Cinna, murdered by the Roman mob after Antony's Forum speech has goaded it into a frenzy (III.iii). Reasons for cutting the scene are understandable. We have not previously met or heard of Cinna the Poet, and he is never mentioned again. The episode impedes the forward movement of the plot. But this death—random, meaningless, horrifyingly undeserved—is as much a result of Caesar's assassination as the dramatically choreographed suicides on the plains of Philippi, and present-day productions are more likely to include it than not.

In the rest of this chapter, discussions of *Julius Caesar* in performance are arranged chronologically for the most part, but they in no way comprise a complete history of the subject.[1] Examples of specific productions have been chosen in part for their contrast. *Julius Caesar* is a many-sided play; just as it has been staged in a number of different ways, it has made different kinds of appeals to its varying audiences.

This variety of technique and appeal is found in the film versions of the play as well as the stage versions, although the films are fewer in number. They will be treated at the end of the chapter.

FROM 1599 TO 1642: DAYLIGHT ON AN OPEN STAGE

Our mental image of the earliest performances of *Julius Caesar* must rely to some extent on the leaps of conjecture taken by scholars. Fortunately, a great deal of information about London's public theaters has survived, and these leaps are taken from fairly solid ground. The replica of Shakespeare's Globe, which opened on London's South Bank in the mid-1990s, has had the benefit of massive scholarly consultation[2] and may be welcomed as an authentic re-creation of Shakespeare's theater in 1599, the year of *Julius Caesar*'s first production.

The Globe resembled a sort of giant doughnut—perhaps three doughnuts stacked on one another, not actually round but so many-sided as to give that impression. The reconstructed Globe, following archaeological investigations, has twenty sides. The roof was thatched, though after the first Globe burned in 1613, the thatch was replaced by tile. The three levels of galleries under the roof held up to twenty-five hundred people, squeezed tightly together on benches, and the open courtyard surrounding the stage provided standing room for five hundred more. The reconstructed Globe, incidentally, although the same size as the original, holds only half that number, partly because of fire regulations and partly because playgoers now are physically larger and more demanding of personal space.[3]

The stage, a large, roofed platform jutting out into the courtyard, was the main acting area. Various smaller acting areas, such as a balcony at the back of the stage and an alcove beneath the balcony, were part of the permanent architecture, the "tiring house" (short for "attiring house," or dressing rooms and general backstage area) behind the main stage.

The shape of the playhouse, combined with the playgoers' high tolerance for being squeezed together, meant that although the audience was quite large, nobody was far from the stage or the action taking place on it. The audience had a sense of identity as a group; as a group, they followed the story and joined in the make-believe. Imagination was required. The stage made no effort to create an illusion of visual reality; the facade of the tiring house was always the facade of the tiring house, never hidden by painted backdrops. Everything was done by suggestion. The actors' voices, gestures, and facial expressions and, above all, the playwright's language told the audience what to imagine.

Scholars have conjectured scene-by-scene descriptions of individual plays, including *Julius Caesar*, as they may have been produced at the Globe.[4] The casting, too, has been approached in a spirit of logical deduction. Richard Burbage, the company's leading player, is thought to have taken the part of Brutus, with the other roles distributed among the rest of the company.[5]

As years went by, and as the Lord Chamberlain's Men became the King's Men with the succession to the throne of James I in 1603, *Julius Caesar* appears to have kept its place in the company's repertoire. The original cast retired or died; others took their places. The company's royal patent was reissued when King James was succeeded by his son Charles I in 1625. The end of the era arrived, however, as the English Civil War moved into an active phase. In 1642 the Puritan faction in Parliament gained enough power to order all the theaters closed. The Globe was pulled down two years later.

BETTERTON TO KEMBLE: INDOORS AND ILLUSIONIST

In 1660 the Commonwealth, established in 1649, ended, and monarchy was restored in the person of Charles II. Theater, now legal again, moved indoors and acquired actresses. The roles of Portia and Calphurnia were now open to women. The new theaters were at first rather small, some in fact being converted tennis courts—at that time, an indoor game. They charged high prices and attracted an intimate and elitist audience. Special effects were much sought after. Many of the staging devices were reminiscent of the court masques of the early seventeenth century, including painted illusionist scenery.

When the tennis court theaters burned down or otherwise became unusable, London's theatrical entrepreneurs set their sights on the kind of theaters then being built in European capitals—increasingly large buildings, with a great deal of auditorium space being given over to luxurious seating arrangements.[6] Stage design was in a sense aimed at the royal box, meant to be occupied by the monarch as chief theatrical patron and situated at the central point in the back of the auditorium. The scenery was created, its perspective lines carefully worked out, to look most convincing when viewed from the royal box. The actors played to that point as well. And since a great gulf of empty air hung between the stage and the royal box, acting technique became broader, slower, and more declamatory, accompanied by large explanatory gestures. (Actors on Shakespeare's stage, scholars assume, spoke rather quickly. Because of the theater's comparatively small dimensions, the audience had no difficulty in following the lines.)

Speaking loudly and slowly had the benefit of reaching the occupants not only of the royal box but of the much cheaper seats in the highest galleries. Actors were well aware of the need to fill the gallery seats if the theater were to stay solvent.

Gallery occupants also had the disruptive habit of shouting down to the stage, should the actors become inaudible.

Julius Caesar seems to have adapted well to these changes. A play filled with public speeches, whose characters in fact talk to one another as if they were making public speeches even in private conversation, would naturally fit the new acting techniques. The theaters' emphasis on visual spectacle also seems made to order for *Julius Caesar*. One can imagine the delight of a scene designer when told to reproduce ancient Rome. Classical building styles had become a leading source of inspiration for seventeenth- and eighteenth-century architects, so that the setting for *Julius Caesar* might have seemed, paradoxically enough, the very latest thing.

From the 1660s until his death in 1710, Thomas Betterton, actor and theater manager, was solidly associated with *Julius Caesar*. He played Brutus, the part generally taken by leading men until the late nineteenth century, and has been described in this role by a contemporary dramatist, Colley Cibber. The reference is to the "quarrel scene" (IV.iii). "When the Betterton Brutus was provoked in his dispute with Cassius, his spirit flew only to his eye; his steady look alone supplied that terror which he disdained an intemperance in his voice should rise to. Thus with a settled dignity of contempt, like an unheeding rock he repelled upon himself the foam of Cassius."[7]

This image of a rock-calm Brutus continued through the eighteenth century and was taken up by John Philip Kemble, leader of the well-known Kemble family of actors, in an 1812 production. Simplified characterization was in vogue not only as a practical acting technique in cavernous theaters and as a way to avoid perplexing an audience with awkward ambiguities, but because it now had an aesthetic theory behind it. Art was expected to emphasize the universal, the ideal; quirky particulars were discouraged. Sir Joshua Reynolds, eighteenth-century painter and for many years president of the Royal Academy of Art, supported this theory, and as a personal friend of Reynolds, Kemble presumably paid careful heed.

The art of painting affected the theater in ways other than theoretical. For *Julius Caesar*, Kemble tried to make the stage look like a historical painting of the heroic school. The scenery aimed for the authentic, although the designers apparently yielded to the anachronistic temptation of depicting imperial Rome, the Rome built by Octavius after he became known as Augustus Caesar, with its marble monuments and temples, rather than the more humble Rome of Julius Caesar. Since historical paintings typically included groups of people scattered about the canvas, Kemble followed suit with between eighty and ninety extras, or "supernumeraries." These, wearing tunics, togas, and sandals, were arranged onstage in carefully balanced patterns or were marched about in processions. There was plenty of room for all this. The theater, Covent Garden, rebuilt several years previously in unprecedented splendor, held over three thousand people, many of them in tiers of comfortable boxes. The stage was of proportions to match.

Shakespeare's text as altered by Kemble has come down to us because Kemble conveniently published it, "adapted to the stage by J. P. Kemble . . . as it is per-

Mr C. KEMBLE as MARC ANTONY.

Pub. as the Act directs, 24th Octr 1826, by D. leh. 27 Bow Str. Covent London.

Charles Kemble (1775–1854), member of a famous English stage dynasty, as an energetic Antony. By permission of the Folger Shakespeare Library.

formed at the Theatres Royal," according to the title page of the 1814 edition.[8] The proscription scene (IV.i) is omitted; thus Antony, played by John Philip Kemble's handsome and popular brother Charles, becomes unambiguously a noble young athlete, determined to revenge his friend, quite lacking in self-interest, and certainly not the kind of person who might cold-bloodedly order the execution of his political enemies. Other of Kemble's cuts emphasize Brutus's calm, philosophical nature. He does not, for example, urge his fellow conspirators to bathe their hands in Caesar's blood (III.i.106).

To make it easier for the audience to keep track of the characters, the text drops a number of them. Murellus and Flavius are replaced by Casca and Trebonius in the opening scene, and minor characters in Acts IV and V are thinned out and their roles combined.

Kemble's production of *Julius Caesar* was highly influential throughout the nineteenth century. It was frequently revived, and Kemble's acting edition of the play was the one to which theater managers regularly turned when contemplating a production of their own.

THE BOOTH FAMILY: TRAGEDY MEETS REALITY

The involvement of the Booth family, a famous American acting dynasty, with Shakespeare's *Julius Caesar* demonstrates the power of this play to work itself into the mental fabric of both a single individual and an entire society. The first and third acts of this strange eventful history are theatrical productions; the second belongs to the realm of history.

On November 25, 1864, New Yorkers had an opportunity to see the three Booth brothers performing on the same stage for the first time in their professional lives. As events turned out, it was also the last. The occasion was a one-night benefit performance of *Julius Caesar*, arranged by a committee celebrating the tercentenary of Shakespeare's birth by raising money for a statue of Shakespeare to be placed in Central Park. (The commission was given to sculptor J.Q.A. Ward and the statue completed in 1870.)

That a cultural project of this sort could flourish in the midst of the American Civil War simply indicates that from the northern perspective, the war was going well. Abraham Lincoln had been reelected several weeks previously. Atlanta had fallen in September, and Sherman was marching through Georgia. Richmond, capital of the Confederacy, still held out, but everyone assumed that victory would come when the spring campaign began. People could think of other things, Shakespeare among them.

The father of the three brothers, Junius Brutus Booth, who had died twelve years previously, had come to America from London in the 1820s and enjoyed a successful acting career despite his tendencies toward both alcoholism and eccentric, in fact sometimes decidedly unbalanced, behavior.[9] His sons kept up family contact as best they could, but as each spent most of his time on tour, they were seldom in the same place at the same time.

The production was a simple one, with the actors as the main attraction. *Julius Caesar* was chosen largely because a Shakespeare play was appropriate, and this one contained the right number of strong parts. Edwin Booth, best known of the three to New Yorkers, played Brutus. Cassius was given to the oldest brother, Junius, who spent most of his time acting in California and other western states. John Wilkes, the youngest, who usually acted and toured in the South, played Antony. John Wilkes was athletic of build, tempestuous of manner, and magnetic in swaying both the Roman crowd and the audience. He was decidedly the hit of the evening. Only later did theater historians find it ironic that "Wilkes Booth should have enacted Antony, friend of law and order as well as of the stricken Caesar."[10]

Richmond fell, and with it the Confederacy, on April 2, 1865. On April 4, President Lincoln visited the city, conferred with the occupying Union officers, and pledged the restoration of Virginia to the Union. He then returned to Washington. On the evening of April 14, Good Friday, as he sat in a box at Ford's Theatre, Lincoln was fatally shot by John Wilkes Booth.

It would seem that Shakespeare's Brutus was in the depths of John Wilkes's mind as he planned and executed the assassination. Eleanor Ruggles, biographer of Edwin Booth, reports a conversation at Edwin Booth's breakfast table the previous November, the day after the brothers had performed *Julius Caesar*. Upon Edwin's mentioning that he had voted for Lincoln's reelection, John Wilkes went into a rage, shouting that "his brother knew not what he had done, that he would live to see Lincoln the king of America."[11]

Timothy Hampton, pointing out another link between John Wilkes Booth and Brutus, suggests that Booth identified with the displaced aristocrats of the South, as Brutus had identified with his aristocratic ancestors. Booth's father's name supplies a further association: "The fact that his [Booth senior's] name was Junius Brutus Booth makes John Wilkes's 'heroic' act an imitation of a Brutus, just as Brutus's own heroism recalls that of his ancestor who drove the Tarquins from Rome."[12]

Written evidence of this psychological connection appears in a pocket diary John Wilkes Booth kept while he was a fugitive, pursued by northerners and southerners alike, in Maryland and Virginia. "I am here in despair," he wrote. "And why? For doing what Brutus was honored for. . . . I struck for my country, and that alone. A country groaned beneath this tyranny and prayed for this end, and yet now behold the cold hand they extend to me."[13]

John Wilkes Booth's personal battle of Philippi arrived on April 26, when Union troops found him hiding in a tobacco barn in the general neighborhood of Rappahannock, Virginia. The co-conspirator who had accompanied him surrendered, but Booth refused to come out, and the barn was set afire. Booth was seen inside, silhouetted by the flames, drawing his revolver. Whether he killed himself, Brutus fashion, or was shot by one of the soldiers is a matter of dispute.

For the third act in the Booth family's connection with *Julius Caesar*, occurring six years later, we return to theater history. There had been some difficult times. Junius Booth, suspected as an accomplice, had been briefly imprisoned. Edwin

Booth as " Brutus."

Edwin Booth (1833–1893), leading American actor in his time, as Brutus. Booth's appearance in this role became controversial after his brother, John Wilkes Booth, assassinated President Lincoln in 1865. By permission of the Folger Shakespeare Library.

Booth had escaped this fate but had left the stage for eight months. When he returned in early 1866, in his best-known role as Hamlet, one of the New York papers had jeered, "Is the assassination of Caesar to be performed? Will Booth appear as the assassin of Caesar? That would be, perhaps, the most suitable character."[14]

Despite such criticisms, most of the public welcomed Booth's return, so much so that within a few years he was able to build his own theater and, in 1871, to mount the most spectacular production of *Julius Caesar* the United States had seen. A few hostile voices were heard. Roger Shattuck cites a "scurrilous sheet" that wondered how Booth could be so morally callous as to stage the "assassination play" and asked how, in his role of Brutus, "he then could have maintained his composure during that awful scene in which, in mockery, he played the part which John Wilkes Booth played with such fearful earnestness, no one but Edwin Booth and God can tell."[15]

It is possible that Booth chose *Julius Caesar* for just this reason. He may have wanted to look his enemy in the face, to proclaim the fact that he and his late brother were separate persons, and that he himself was innocent. Perhaps, too, he hoped to make the point that *Julius Caesar*, regardless of historical parallels, might also be seen simply as a play being performed on a stage—in this case, seen elaborately as a play being performed on a stage, for the physical surroundings were very impressive indeed.

Booth's Theatre, a massive edifice filled with marble, gilt, gaslight chandeliers, and every provision for luxury and comfort, delighted the public and fulfilled its expectations of stagecraft as magical illusion.[16] For *Julius Caesar*, Booth made use of everything he had. His scenic designer, Charles Witham, created a series of sets that reproduced imperial Rome (the usual and expected anachronism) on a massive scale. Members of the audience who kept up with the art world noted that Witham had based his design for the interior of the Capitol on a well-known painting by the French academician Jean-Léon Gérome, *La Mort de César*, following Gérome's composition for the grouping of the figures but greatly expanding the architectural magnitude. The set was populated by hundreds of extras, including women and children—this last an unusual touch at the time.

Julius Caesar ran for almost three months, considerably longer than expected. Eventually, for reasons having to do with the actors' previous commitments, Booth shifted from the role of Brutus to that of Cassius and then to Antony. This variation extended the play's run, as the audience kept returning in order to compare Booth's interpretations of his respective roles. The production was revived several times, using the same scenery though usually with different actors, and Booth later arranged similar though less elaborate productions of *Julius Caesar* to take on tour.

From the standpoint of theater history, Booth's 1871 *Julius Caesar* was not so much a new thing as a continuation of the pattern that Kemble had set decades earlier. It relied on spectacle for much of its effect; the text was cut in order to simplify the action; ambiguities in character were smoothed out. The production should be evaluated in the context of its time, however. In Ripley's words, Booth's goal was "the use of visual splendor to enhance the spiritual and emotional impact of the acting. The soul, he hoped, might be reached through the senses. His settings . . . often achieved a poetic dimension which went beyond their surface realism and commanded attention as painterly compositions in their own right."[17]

In America, Booth's *Julius Caesar* can be taken as representative of the high-water mark of this particular aesthethic goal, a goal that in the twentieth century was to be condemned as old-fashioned and even un-Shakespearean. In England, where the economy by the turn of the century had reached a more flourishing state than even in America, the high-water mark was to be more lavish yet.

BEERBOHM TREE AND THE LAST HURRAH OF EMPIRE

In the summer of 1897, the Diamond Jubilee of Queen Victoria filled the streets of London with pageantry, glamour, camels, elephants, pashas in turbans and diamonds, regiments of Sikhs, headhunters from Borneo, and all the exotic exuberance that an enormous and wealthy empire could muster.[18] The festivities were of special interest to Herbert Beerbohm Tree, ebullient actor and manager of Her Majesty's Theatre.[19] Pondering the question of his next production, and always attuned to the mood of his audience, he decided on *Julius Caesar*, to open in January 1898.

Tree is unlikely to have set out systematically to go Booth's production one better, as he had not seen the New York *Julius Caesar* and as his competition by way of spectacular Shakespeare came from such London venues as Henry Irving's Lyceum Theatre. Still, one almost gets that impression. Tree's scene designer, for instance, instead of seeking inspiration in the work of famous painters of historical canvases, was himself a famous painter of historical canvases, Lawrence Alma-Tadema, known for his portrayals of ancient Egypt and Greece but especially for those of Rome. Again, where Booth had grouped his extras ("supernumeraries") about the stage in picturesque but rather static groups, Tree galvanized his into action. The opening scene became a lively panorama of dancing girls, children at play, and athletes warming up for the Lupercalian games. All these activities were well under way before the cobbler and his friends are called on to defend their holiday making, or Caesar's vast procession makes its way onto the stage.

The Roman populace was a much-emphasized component of the production. Tree makes this point in an article he wrote for a souvenir program: "At Her Majesty's it is not the historic band of conspirators that strikes the key note of the play. It is not even the mighty figure of Caesar, treacherously brought low. It is the feverish, pulsing life of the eternal city."[20]

Here Tree implies definite parallels between Rome and London, and between ancient Romans and contemporary Londoners. London in 1898 considered itself a city of feverish and pulsing life, the center of a mighty empire. Comfortably seated in Tree's theater, the audience could enjoy a special sense of rapport with events onstage. Contemporary parallels were taken even further. Ralph Berry suggests a link between Julius Caesar and Queen Victoria, not in any physical sense but from the perspective of dignity, responsibility, and especially the exemplifying of upright morality. Tree's souvenir program continues with the observation that Roman life reflected the Romans' "boundless wealth and indescribable extravagance. . . . The once hardy, abstemious mode of living soon degenerated into grossness and sensuality." Londoners presumably recognized themselves here, or perhaps recognized the London that might evolve were it not for the salutory role of Queen Victoria and the rest of the royal family, reigning through high-minded duty and inspiring their subjects' return to old-fashioned values. As Berry puts it, Tree's production postulates that "if Rome is luxurious and decadent, Caesar is a benign reformist and sorely needed dictator."[21]

Tree's *Julius Caesar* was revived several times during the following decades, when the heads of empire became successively Edward VII and George V. The souvenir program just quoted. in fact, was written for a revival of the play timed for the coronation of George V in 1911. It might perhaps indicate Tree's hope that his vision of a parallel Rome and London would continue under the new sovereign.

Tree's conversion of Caesar into an imperially correct dramatic centerpiece meant that the assassins became villains of even deeper dye, and Brutus lost his claim to even potentially heroic status. This shift would seem to pose a problem for an actor-manager accustomed to playing the lead. Tree solved it by making Antony the hero and taking this role.

Among the textual cuts was the proscription scene (IV.i). Antony's motives must be above suspicion. Aside from cutting the text, Tree further emphasized Antony's role by his division of the play into three acts. Each act gave Antony the closing speech and a "tableau," what a modern audience might call a freeze-frame as the curtain falls, an effect dear to Victorian playgoers' hearts.

The first act of Tree's production takes the plot through the assassination of Caesar and closes as Antony vows revenge. Calphurnia then silently enters—an innovation on Tree's part—and mourns over her husband's body, while Antony stands protectively beside her. As Ripley points out, "The avenger of callous murder we have seen before; the champion of the widow is a novel, even unique, variant."[22]

Tree's second act consisted entirely of the Forum scene (III.ii). Its spectacular effect resulted not only from the visual grandeur of the scenery, which included reconstructions of the temples of Saturn, Jupiter, and Concord, but from the energy and movement of the crowd of extras during Brutus's and Antony's speeches. These reactions seemed to be spontaneous but had actually been carefully choreographed. From a political standpoint, the crowd's ultimate support of Caesar's cause implied that an emperor's authority is derived from the people he rules—a theory that might have puzzled the historical Julius Caesar but that presumably pleased Tree's audience—Queen Victoria's "beloved people," as she had addressed them on Jubilee Day the previous summer.[23] The Forum scene, and also the second act, end as the citizens hurry away and Antony, alone on stage, urges the personification of mischief to "take thou what course thou wilt" (III.ii.260).

The announcement of Octavius's arrival, immediately following in Shakespeare's text, is omitted, as is the mob's killing of Cinna the Poet. Simplifying the action and keeping the focus on Antony would seem the purpose of these and other cuts. The fate of Cinna also shows the Roman crowd in an inconveniently bad light.

Tree's third act, rushing through the remaining episodes, gave little emphasis to either the quarrel between Brutus and Cassius or the appearance of Caesar's ghost. Battle scenes were energetically performed to stirring music from the orchestra, but the suicides were not prolonged, and much of the text was cut. At the end, a textual transposition gave Antony the closing words, so once again he could strike an effective pose as the curtain fell.

Neither Tree nor his audience realized it, but the curtain was soon to fall as well on both the concepts so energetically embodied in this *Julius Caesar*. Elaborately staged Shakespeare—hundreds of extras, dazzling illusionist sets—would become a thing of the past within a few decades, although to some extent the tradition has persisted in the cinema. And Tree's view of Julius Caesar as an unambiguously gracious and nonthreatening autocrat would soon be out of step with fashionable political ideals. Occasionally now a director will associate Shakespeare's Caesar with some relatively sympathetic figure, perhaps a victim of assassination currently in the public eye. Usually, however, the parallel is decidedly negative.

ORSON WELLES AND THE FASCIST CAESAR

Orson Welles's 1937 New York production of *Julius Caesar* made a great splash because of its link with current events, startlingly explicit for that time and not what audiences were used to, and also because of its staging. England had been experimenting since the turn of the century with the Shakespearean techniques advocated by innovator William Poel and others, ideas including an open stage with simple or no scenery, a constant flow of action without pauses between scenes, and an uncut text.[24] In America, the old pattern of lavish and slow-moving Shakespeare seems to have died more slowly, but by the 1930s the public had become accustomed to artistic upheavals in various fields and was willing to take a chance on the work of this child prodigy—Welles was only twenty-two—who had gained a reputation for theatrical daring. Welles's "voodoo Macbeth" the previous year had defied tradition by using black actors and hypnotically rhythmic music.

In adopting the new techniques, Welles picked and chose, attempting not so much a return to the theater of Shakespeare as an onward journey, seeking a theatrical form suited to his own time and to what he wanted to say. He did not try to use the full text; his cutting, in fact, was drastic. The set, a complicated assortment of bare platforms connected by stairs and ramps, allowed a constant flow of movement, in accordance with Poel's principles but also in accordance with Welles's desire for a relentlessly driving pace.

Costumes were modern. John Houseman, who was closely involved with the production, describes their purpose:

> To emphasize the similarity between the last days of the Roman Republic and
> the political climate in Europe in the mid-thirties, our Roman aristocrats wore
> military uniforms that suggested but did not exactly reproduce the current
> fashion of the Fascist ruling class; our crowd wore the dark, nondescript street
> clothes of the big-city proletariat.[25]

Although the military uniforms were intended as a reference to fascist power in
general, the actor playing Caesar, Joseph Holland, happened to have a massive
lower jaw and was immediately identified by audience and critics with Mussolini.

Welles took the part of Brutus, interpreting the character, in Welles's words, as
"the classical picture of the eternal, impotent, ineffective, fumbling liberal; the re-
former who wants to do something about things but doesn't know how."[26] This figure of the liberal thinker, dismayed but powerless, was one with which many
members of the audience could identify in 1937. The times were out of joint in
many ways. The worst of the Great Depression was over, but life was not back to
what people preferred to consider normal. In Europe, ominous events were piling
up. Hitler with his Nazi party and Mussolini with his Black Shirts had solidified
their respective dictatorships in German and Italy. Each had territorial ambitions.
Mussolini had just conquered Ethiopia, then known as Abyssinia; Hitler was jug-
gling treaties in preparation for expanding the German borders, seeking living
space for what he considered the naturally superior Aryan race. In recognition of
their similar aims and methods, Hitler and Mussolini had the previous year established the Berlin-Rome Axis, a loose understanding that would become a formal
alliance in 1939.

To suggest this atmosphere of suddenly breaking events, dramatic headlines,
and urgent radio broadcasts, Welles used sound effects both subtle and startling.
The actors' footfalls echoed on the wooden platforms with the connotation of
armies marching relentlessly across Europe. A musical score composed by Marc
Blitzstein used trumpet, percussion, and Hammond organ to underline the play's
dynamic rhythm. Houseman also recalls "the deep booming of a huge, old-fashioned thunder drum."[27]

Visual effects imitated newsreels and news photographs, in those days almost
always shot in black and white. The play's subdued color scheme was set off by a
deep red background, painted onto the bare bricks at the back of the stage. *Julius
Caesar*'s lighting had the stark effect of flashbulbs. Characters would enter the action by stepping into a shaft of light and exit by disappearing into a shadow. One
type of light was set into the floor of the stage and shone straight upward; the cast
referred to these as the "Nuremberg lights," a term that may need explanation
since this German town is now known for the trials of former Nazi leaders held
there in 1945–1946. In 1937, the public associated Nuremberg with the annual rallies sponsored by Hitler and his associates, propaganda exercises with games, pa-
rades, and policy speeches, all thoroughly covered by the media. A reviewer in
Time magazine specifically mentioned this link, suggesting that the lighting of
Welles's production was "patterned after *Life* [magazine]'s pictures of last sum-

mer's Nazi Congress at Nuremberg, vertical shafts of light stabbing up through the darkness."[28]

A direct association with the Nuremberg rallies informs what became the pivotal scene in Welles's production: the killing of Cinna the Poet. Two years previously, at the 1935 rally, Hitler had announced legislation reducing German Jews to second-class citizens, subject to restrictions in mobility and choice of profession. Considerable violence against Jews had followed. In the words of Norman Lloyd, who played Cinna the Poet, his character's fate "symbolized what was happening in the world, if your name was Greenberg—and even if you weren't Jewish."[29]

Cinna's death, staged quietly as the persecutors emerge from the shadows to form a ring about the wide-eyed, gentle poet, had an overwhelming effect on the audience. Some of this effect may have been due to novelty; the scene was so regularly omitted in performance that people were not used to seeing it.

The text in general, however, was severely cut, partly to shorten and simplify the action and partly to emphasize the role of Brutus. Acts IV and V were shrunk to a bare sketch. The death of Cinna the Poet (III.iii) is followed immediately by the quarrel scene (IV.ii) between Brutus and Cassius. Caesar's ghost is omitted. Brutus's servant Lucius, when asked for music, obliges with a poignant song taken from Shakespeare's and Fletcher's *Henry VIII*, "Orpheus with his Lute," part of Lucius's repertoire in many productions of *Julius Caesar*. The lights dim, military music symbolizes a battle, and the lights come up as Brutus stands beside Cassius's body. Brutus then kills himself, and Antony enters to eulogize him. Octavius Caesar, having been cut from the play entirely, does not appear.

Other textual changes enhance Brutus's image as a man of thoughtful, nonviolent integrity. Brutus does not urge his companions to bathe their hands in Caesar's blood (III.i.105); he tells Cassius of Portia's death but does not hear the news again from Messala (IV.iii.189); and he does not do an about-fact on the question of committing suicide if captured (V.i.103–112).

The sweep of the action was powerful and audiences were enthusiastic. According to a reviewer:

> Manhattan playgoers took the play's smooth unmetered flow, its indubitable 1937 flavor, with mingled delight and disbelief. The delight was for a first-rate show that, played straight ahead with no break, kept them on the edges of their seats for an hour and forty minutes. The disbelief arose from the snobbish, traditional feeling that Shakespeare must be dressed up fit to kill, cannot possibly be made presentable on the bare boards he wrote for.[30]

STAGE PRODUCTIONS IN THE LAST HALF OF THE TWENTIETH CENTURY

Welles's *Julius Caesar* made so vivid an impression on theatergoers, and on theater makers, that a perceived need to relate the play to the audience's own political world has become dominant and almost inescapable in productions of the play.

Julius Caesar in modern dress. Calphurnia (Tricia Kelley) tries her persuasive arts on Caesar (David Sumner). Stratford-upon-Avon, 1993. Reproduced by courtesy of the Shakespeare Centre Library, Stratford-upon-Avon.

This concept is not necessarily a departure from the play's intention. The possibility of various interpretations is implied in the text and verbalized by Cassius:

> How many ages hence
> Shall this our lofty scene be acted over
> In states unborn and accents yet unknown? (III.i.111–113)

The following brief survey of recent productions seeks only to point out trends in the staging of *Julius Caesar* and to give a few examples illustrating these trends. It is in no way complete. For a fuller view, readers are referred to several books on Shakespearean stage history and to periodicals that regularly print reviews of Shakespearean productions. Ripley's *Julius Caesar on Stage*, cited frequently in this chapter, discusses productions through 1973. Langdon Brown covers the period 1950 through 1983 in the *Julius Caesar* section, pp. 257–281, of *Shakespeare Around the Globe: A Guide to Notable Postwar Revivals*, ed. Samuel L. Leiter (Westport, Conn.: Greenwood Press, 1986). Essays on the play's stage history by Roy Walker, Richard David, Ralph Berry, and Sylvan Barnett appear in the Signet Classics edition of *Julius Caesar* (1987), pp. 216–245. Marvin Spevack gives a brief but lively theatrical survey in his New Cambridge edition of *Julius Caesar* (1988), pp. 31–45. Finally, current productions are reviewed in most issues of *Shakespeare Bulletin* and *Shakespeare Quarterly*; this last periodical also puts out the annual *World Shakespeare Bibliography*, which lists theater reviews as well as scholarship. Easily available indexes for theater reviews include the *Readers Guide* and the indexes to the *New York Times* and the *Times* of London.

Besides bringing in political references, today's stage productions seek to build bridges to the audience in numerous ways. Costumes, stage effects, and attempts to merge the audience with the Roman plebeians are among these strategies. An emphasis on the women characters appeals to present-day sensibilities; this concept sometimes extends to nontraditional casting in which women play parts written for men. Black and other minority actors often appear. In addition, many productions manage to combine contemporary political reference with an exploration of character, so that the play becomes a study in friendship, envy, one-upmanship and other aspects of human nature that, though timeless, have a special appeal to audiences interested in questions of psychology and personality.

Caesar's dictatorial identities can vary considerably. Recent history has provided a choice of models. It should be noted that linking Caesar with some modern dictator or other does not necessarily mean the loss of the play's ambiguity, although a certain amount of simplification may take place. As always, a more sympathetic Caesar means a more villainous conspiracy, and vice versa.

In productions mounted in the United States, South America and adjacent regions have been a popular choice of locale. The Guthrie Theatre in Minneapolis set a 1969 production in a generalized Latin American dictatorship; the stage design featured a huge Mayan idol, bringing in the idea of past as well as current oppressive regimes.[31]

In 1986, a Miami production titled *Julio Cesar* made use of anti-Castro sentiment, with a bearded Caesar wearing army fatigues and smoking a cigar. Characters greeted one another in Spanish and gathered to conspire at sidewalk cafés. A
Haitian actress played the Soothsayer as a *santera*, or voodoo sorceress, prophesy-
ing and chanting. After the assassination, the conspirators hacked Caesar's body
with machetes.[32]

Another of Caesar's South American excursions was staged by the Philadelphia
Drama Guild in 1988. According to reviewer Cary Mazer, the play's being set in a
"post-colonial multi-ethnic society" allowed the production to become "a show-
case for black and hispanic actors."[33] Casting was nontraditional in other ways as
well. Metellus Cimber was turned into a woman ("Metella Cimber"), carried
through into Acts IV and V, supplied with Titinius's lines, and romantically linked
to Cassius. As Mazer observes, "Giving Cassius a love interest may neutralize the
implicit homoeroticism of the male-bonding between Brutus and Cassius, but it
does give Mettela a splendid, and grandly romantic, suicide scene."

Among European dictators, Mussolini and Hitler continue to serve as easily rec-
ognizable parallels to Caesar, as Welles had demonstrated. In 1993, a production
at Stratford-upon-Avon, Warwickshire, found a new twist by giving Calphurnia a
striking similarity to Raisa Gorbachev, wife of Russian leader Mikhail S. Gorbachev. Rather confusingly from the standpoint of marital consistency, reviewers
also identified this production's Caesar with Romanian dictator Nicolae Ceau-
sescu. Communication technology was also in evidence; Caesar's entry in I.ii was
accompanied by a television camera.[34]

High-tech devices frequently find their way into updated versions of *Julius Caesar*; computers, portable telephones, and audiocassette players accompany the
characters' various rhetorical undertakings. A giant video screen, placed upstage
behind the actors, magnified the speakers' faces and gave an effect of instant public significance in a 1983 production at Stratford-upon-Avon.[35]

Costuming in *Julius Caesar* is a matter of special concern to directors. The traditional togas may harbor unwanted connotations of Turkish baths, for example, or
American fraternity parties. Modern dress offers itself as one solution, as does any
form of period costume that allows easily readable distinctions of rank and personality. A Stratford, Ontario, production of 1990 found a compromise: "Dazzling
white togas are worn for formal occasions, but plainly visible beneath are always
the modern (or pseudo-modern) jogging pants, sweatshirts, and turtlenecks of the
more personal or secretive scenes."[36] A 1991 Stratford-upon-Avon production
blended costumes inspired by Renaissance Italy, in rich reds and blues, with contemporary touches; Antony wore dark leather, while the battle scenes combined
"the helmets, sandbags, and trench dikes of World War I" with "the spears and
shields of ancient Rome."[37]

Some productions make a point of simplicity in costumes, settings, and special
effects generally. In 1987, Terry Hands impressed Stratford-upon-Avon audiences
and reviewers with the economy of his approach:

The production appeared almost static compared with the lavish use of revolving scenery and agitated crowds which has become the dominant fashion.
With all the space available, the actors hardly move from the apron and address most of their speeches directly to the audience. This mode of delivery
makes for clarity. It is also a test of performance, cruelly underlining even
minor defects. . . . Roger Allen as Brutus effortlessly brings out the beauty and
meaning of each line as if he just let Shakespeare's text breathe through him,
but Sean Baker overacts and turns Cassius into a vulgar thug.[38]

In another gesture toward relevance, directors often urge the theater audience to
identify themselves with the Roman mob, especially in the Forum scene (III.ii)
with its display of large-scale persuasive techniques reminiscent of political cam-
paigns. The actors playing the mob may enter from the back of the auditorium, for
example, and shout their responses to Brutus's and Antony's speeches while standing or sitting in the aisles. In a 1977 production at London's National Theatre, "the
crowd's omnipresence drew the audience into the play," according to critics.[39] The
1993 Stratford-upon-Avon production, besides evoking the ambience of twentieth-
century Eastern Europe, also employed promenade staging, in which the audience
actually occupied the acting area and could wander about among the performers.
This unaccustomed liberty became something of a hazard during the battle scenes,
for "the audience is forced to dodge about nervously, second-guessing the direction of the next onslaught, in case they should get in the way of the very loud, and
very energetically staged, fighting."[40]

Nontraditional casting was emphasized in Corin Redgrave's 1996 production at
Houston's Alley Theatre. A critic commented of Howard Saddler's Cassius that the
line "I was born free as Caesar" (I.ii.97) "assumed added import spoken by a man
of African heritage."[41] Antony was played by black actor David Harewood, who
continued the role in *Antony and Cleopatra*, with Vanessa Redgrave as Cleopatra,
in this dual collaborative effort of the Alley Theatre and London's Moving Theatre
Company.

Actors and directors interested in nuances of characterization are often led to a
more sensitive treatment of Cassius. As early as 1950, John Gielgud's interpretation at Stratford-upon-Avon impressed critics. "Cassius was allowed a measure of
nobility. No longer merely a passionate foil to Brutus's tranquility, Gielgud's lean
and hungry Roman emerged as the coiled spring which vitalizes the tragedy."[42]
Gielgud was to play Cassius in a more permanent form several years later, in the
Mankiewicz film of *Julius Caesar*. Again, Patrick Stewart's 1972 Cassius struck
observers as "a red-blooded individualist, impatient of restriction."[43]

Antony, another complex character the exploration of whose multiple facets is of
interest to audiences now, was played by Al Pacino in a New York Shakespeare Festival production of 1988. "Pacino's Antony is the show-stopper. . . . At the beginning, his shy smile is perfect for a young and deferential local politician, one who
seems to come from the wrong side of the tracks. It's not long before we realize that
it is Antony, the runner and bon vivant, who is ambitious rather than Caesar."[44]

Interpretations of Julius Caesar himself tend to present the character as either smaller than life, so that his pretensions become ironic, or larger than life, so that he really is what he says he is. Christopher Benjamin's 1995 small-scale Caesar contrasted literally with his own image as evoked by the stage design. "Presumably the point is that the man is less than the pretence. . . . That idea is emphasized by the eight-foot-high marble head that dominates the beginning and the ending. . . . But it is hard to imagine this podgy man-mattress routing Goths or crossing Rubicons."[45]

A contrastingly large-scale Caesar, central to the play even after his assassination, appeared in a 1957 production at Stratford-upon-Avon. Caesar, played by Cyril Luckham, was represented after his death by the "northern star" to which Caesar had compared his own constancy (III.i.60). This stage effect appeared shining serenely over the Forum when Antony cried, "Here was a Caesar! When comes such another?" (ii.252); it shone over the body of Cinna the Poet and appeared again in the last act, when Brutus cried, "O Julius Caesar, thou art mighty yet" (V.iii.94).[46] Roy Walker has described his own scholarly participation in this effect. He mentioned to the director, Glen Byam Shaw, the passage in Ovid's *Metamorphoses* in which Caesar's body is carried by Venus into the heavens and becomes a star (Book XV). Walker modestly adds, "But a suggested interpretation is one thing; imaginative transformation is another. Mr. Byam Shaw transmuted the argument into his own art."[47]

FILM VERSIONS

Unquestionably, a film version of any play lacks the immediacy and electricity of a stage performance. Actors onstage are creating a work of art before the audience's eyes, and the result is unique. No single performance is identical to any other single performance. The audience, responding immediately to whatever is happening onstage, becomes an intrinsic part of the event, for actors claim that they are influenced, from moment to moment, by this response of the audience.

Yet a filmed version of a play has its own appeal. It is not as ephemeral as an evening's stage performance, and will not vanish—or, at least, will not vanish as quickly; the ultimate impermanence of the various film technologies, with the possible exception of digital recording, is a distressing fact of life. However, for as long as they do manage to endure, films serve as a record, and they can be visited over and over, like books in fact.

Julius Caesar has been filmed fairly often, in part or as a whole. Forty entries appear in the *Julius Caesar* section of Kenneth Rothwell's and Annabelle Henkin Melzer's film bibliography, *Shakespeare on Screen*.[48] Of these, some are available only in archives, some have been lost, and some exist only as fragments, but as a group they represent a great deal of cinematic and Shakespearean energy. In 1911, for example, a ten-minute silent film was made to record parts of a production of *Julius Caesar* by the F. R. Benson acting company, a group famous for its simple and straightforward presentation of Shakespeare. Another ten-minute *Julius Cae-*

sar was made in 1937 and transmitted in one of the earliest BBC (British Broadcasting Company) programs on Shakespeare; the ten minutes consisted of Antony's oration in the Forum (III.ii).

In 1949, an independent low-budget *Julius Caesar* won the best film award at the Locarno (Switzerland) Film Festival and opened doors to Hollywood for two of the cast: David Bradley, who produced and directed the film and also played Brutus, and Charlton Heston, who played Antony (a role he would repeat in a film discussed later in this chapter). The film was made in and around Chicago, in particular Northwestern University, for the astonishingly low sum of $15,000 (although we must remember that most prices of 1949 would strike us as astonishing).

Among the films made to record various stage productions of *Julius Caesar* is a videotape made at the Delacorte Theatre in Central Park, during the New York Shakespeare Festival of 1979. The cast was all black or Hispanic. Jaime Sanchez played Antony; the director was Michael Langham and the producer Joseph Papp.

Besides *Shakespeare on Screen*, numerous reference and critical works are available for those interested in Shakespeare film.[49] Other material can be found in learned journals and the mass-circulation media.[50]

The remainder of this chapter will be devoted to films of *Julius Caesar* that are readily available on videotape or laser videodisc. Their booklike convenience, since they can be watched whenever the viewer chooses and can also be stopped and started at any point, makes them well suited both for private study and classroom discussion.

The Mankiewicz *Julius Caesar*, 1953

The 1953 Metro-Goldwyn-Mayer *Julius Caesar* was produced by John Houseman, who had been closely associated with the 1937 Orson Welles stage production. The film was shot in black and white, a carryover of sorts from Welles's nearly monochromatic design. There were no overt anachronisms, however. The actors wore togas, and the sets were intended to convey ancient Rome. Director Joseph Mankiewicz put the emphasis on character and story. A musical score by Miklos Rozsa created fulsome background emotion and provided themes for the major characters.

The cast included Marlon Brando as Antony; James Mason as Brutus; and John Gielgud as Cassius. These actors were then in the prime of their careers and worked with vigor and a strong sense of craft. Louis Calhern, as Caesar, belonged to an older generation but possessed a solid screen presence. Deborah Kerr, as Portia, and Greer Garson, as Calphurnia, had necessarily briefer roles but interpreted them with poise and with a recognizably 1950s brand of Hollywood glamour.

The film's authority, energy, and air of cinematic abundance made an immediate and positive impact on public and critics alike. Rome became a place of sweeping visual vistas, with grandiose buildings, statues, and flights of stairs. Roman plebeians thronged the streets. Dogs and goats dashed through the crowds, and water ran in the gutters. John Gielgud, brought up in the traditions of the British

theater, found in Mankiewicz's realistically orchestrated spectacle a certain historical familiarity: "Herbert [Beerbohm] Tree's ghost must have breathed approval,"
Gielgud is reported to have said.[51]

With regard to acting technique, screen actors have an advantage over actors in
large theaters (such as Tree's), in that regardless of the magnitude of their set, they
still have no need to shout their lines; the camera can always close in, moving flu-
idly from panorama to close-up. The audience can then see the subtlest emotions
on an actor's face. At the same time, since the actor has been established as occupying a specific and usually rather large space, the audience feels no sense of
claustrophobia whenever the screen is filled with a single face.

Of the faces in this film, Brutus's is perhaps the most haunting. James Mason's
large, dark eyes and sensitive mouth transmit sympathy and concern. When the
Soothsayer, here played as a blind man with staff and bells, has warned Caesar
about the Ides of March (I.ii.18), Brutus tries to help him get out of the way of the
crowd. The Soothsayer runs his fingers over Brutus's face; while Brutus silently
expresses his pity and desire to help, the Soothsayer becomes aware of his identity
and, presumably because he knows Brutus's future, reacts with horror.

The Soothsayer is correct. For this Brutus, it is not enough to be calm, thoughtful, and kind in such small-scale interactions as helping strangers in a crowd.
When the situation becomes more complex, Mason's Brutus goes into a stall.
Again and again the Mankiewicz film shows him literally backing away from a
problem. We see Brutus's face, still tender and concerned, still declaring Brutus's
nobility and justifying Brutus's actions, but receding from whatever reality is
under way.

John Gielgud's Cassius is a man of vital, focused energy. His tousled hair almost crackles. His gestures are large, though controlled, and his body language
seems to hurl him forward through space and time. Persuading Brutus to join the
assassins, Cassius leans toward him, as if aiming some ray of volition at his reluc-
tant companion. When Brutus takes over the conspiracy and overrules Cassius's
more practical ideas, Cassius's energy turns in on itself, until he seems to jump up
and down inside his skin. During the quarrel scene (IV.iii), Cassius becomes so
angry he trembles all over. This shrewd, strong, and aggressive Cassius seems
aware of the paradoxical weakness in his own need for Brutus's approval, but he is
unable to resolve the contradiction.

Marlon Brando's Mark Antony becomes the pivotal point of the film. John
Houseman compares this production to Welles's stage version, in which Brutus
predominated: "The casting of Marlon Brando as Antony completely reversed the
structure of the play. Now it was Mark Antony they were rooting for and the twelve
hundred cheering bit players and extras massed on M.G.M.'s Stage 25 were merely
reflecting the empathy of future audiences."[52]

Brando's Antony embodies the play's ambiguity, and in a consistent and believable
way. His physical prowess is intrinsic to his personality. In his first appearance, he is
stripped for the Lupercalian games, but even at other times he manages to wear a
more revealing toga than anyone else. This casual and very physical self-assurance

allows him to relate to the other characters from a position of physical and mental strength; unlike Cassius, he does not need anybody else. It bolsters Brando's interpretation that Octavius, played by Douglas Watson, is not emphasized in this film, so that one is not conscious of him as a serious rival for Brando's power.

Antony's relationship with Caesar, in Brando's interpretation, seems touched with an almost ironic tolerance by a young man for an older one—a sort of noblesse oblige. In I.ii, when Caesar asks Antony to touch Calphurnia in the upcoming race and thus magically make her fertile, Antony's knowing, sultry glance at Calphurnia suggests a comparison between himself and Caesar that is hardly flattering to Caesar. Yet there is in Brando's expression a kind of sympathy—perhaps for Caesar, perhaps for Calphurnia.

In his Forum speech (III.ii), a tour de force, Antony revels in working up the crowd, although his sorrow and affection for Caesar seem genuine. At the end of the speech, as the crowd rages and the mutiny gets under way, a close-up catches Antony's private smile. Antony's concluding words, spoken to himself, "Mischief, thou art afoot, / Take thou what course thou wilt" (260–261), originally included in the shooting script, were cut because, according to Jorgens, "Brando's sardonic smile says it all."[53]

The play's final lines are readjusted to give Antony the last words in his eulogy of Brutus: "This was the noblest Roman of them all" (V.v.68). Again, Antony seems to express a genuine feeling of admiration despite the fact that his eulogy directly contradicts what he said about Brutus in his Forum speech. As an athlete, presumably, this Antony would value a victory over an esteemed opponent more than over a trivial one; thus, having won the victory, he upgrades it by esteeming the opponent.

Throughout the film, symbols and emblems abound. Carved eagles, symbolic of Rome, are carried about on standards, and a larger-than-life statue of Caesar watches as Cassius sets out to persuade Brutus that a mere mortal is taking up too much space (I.ii.135–138). Later, Brutus becomes aware of the ghost of Caesar after a small lamp on his table begins to sputter (IV.iii.275). A similar lamp is placed at the head of Brutus's dead body; after Antony speaks his final words, the flame goes out.

The small harp belonging to Lucius, Brutus's young servant, becomes a symbol of innocence and perhaps, as well, of the gentle and sympathetic relationship between this master and servant. We see Lucius playing the harp in IV.iii; later, during the battle, a soldier finds it, broken, in the rubble and takes it to Octavius, who glances at it and throws it away. We assume that Lucius too has come to an unfortunate end.

Another innocent victim of the play's havoc would have been Cinna the Poet (III.iii). This scene not only existed in the original script but was actually shot. It was not used, however. Running time may have been a consideration here; the total is just at two hours, a good maximum for a film designed for general release. Jorgens has also suggested that Mankiewicz may have decided the scene did not sufficiently propel the plot.[54] Other cuts may have been made for this or other reasons. Portia does not tell of wounding her thigh, for example (II.i.299–301); for the dignified Deborah Kerr, such an action would have given her image a considerable jolt.

Dialogue in the battle scenes is condensed, and some of the minor characters are cut or combined with one another. Here the film allows so much more than a stage would, by way of real horses and large-scale dashings about, that the story can be conveyed without a great deal of conversation. Titinius's suicide is eliminated, and the text is rearranged so that Brutus discovers Cassius's body just before he kills himself.

The proscription scene (IV.i), typically cut in productions that choose to simplify Antony's many-sided character, is an effective part of this drama. The three triumvirs plan the deaths of their various enemies while seated comfortably in Caesar's house, the same setting in which, earlier, the conspirators had gathered to escort Caesar to the Capitol (II.ii). The room is elegantly furnished, with a view over the Roman hills and a statue of Caesar still in place. After his companions leave, Antony goes to the window, stretches indolently, looks thoughtfully at Caesar's carved image, and then sits in Caesar's chair.

This film's lack of overt political overtones has not prevented viewers from seeing implicit ones. Roger Manvell finds echoes of Nazi Germany in the mass rallies of the early scenes and in the many images of the leader—in this case, statues rather than posters.[55] Robert F. Willson, Jr., has argued that this *Julius Caesar* makes a special effort to show the Roman mob in a positive light. "Such an interpretation recontextualizes Shakespeare's hierarchal . . . views, placing the film squarely in a 1950s American setting defined by democratic values and fearful of the threat to those values posed by McCarthyism and militarism."[56] The Forum scene, Willson suggests, depicts "the common man's potential nobility. . . . Several citizens are shot in closeup; many appear to be standing on plinths, as if they were statues representing the dignity of their class." And Willson sees another angle to the omission of Cinna the Poet: "The cut ensures that the movie's audience will retain a more sympathetic impression of the Roman mob."

Charlton Heston as Antony, 1969

Charlton Heston's *Julius Caesar*, sixteen years later, made a negative impression on critics. Howard Thompson in the *New York Times* called it "as flat and juiceless as a dead herring"; Kenneth Rothwell says that to him "the film remains something of a mystery since everyone connected with it . . . had enjoyed previous successes on stage and film. Yet it is undeniably stillborn."[57]

Nevertheless, the production has its strong points. Although textual cuts are heavy, the action is brisk. The director, Stuart Burge, had considerable experience with Shakespeare and seems to have had definite effects in mind. Charlton Heston acts Antony with conviction and intensity. John Gielgud, as Caesar, displays his usual mastery, giving the character a human and sympathetic rather than a pompous dimension. Jason Robards plays Brutus; Richard Johnson, Cassius; Diana Rigg, Portia; and Jill Bennet, Calphurnia.

Perhaps in reaction to Mankiewicz's black and white, the Heston film is shot in bright color. The effect, though gaudy, is convenient. The different-colored togas are a great help in telling the characters apart, particularly in the assassination scene (III.i). This scene, in fact, has suffered less from cutting than many of the others. Caius Ligarius has been excised entirely, but most of the dialogue has been kept and the camera work makes clear who is doing what to whom. At one point, the camera looks at the blurred figures through the dying eyes of Caesar.

The Forum scene (III.ii) contrasts the cold formality of Robards's Brutus with the passionate sincerity of Heston's Antony. Antony begins in a large, rhetorical style, as if he were addressing the universe; when he descends from the pulpit (a flight of stairs) to describe Caesar's wounds, he shifts into a more intimate mode and seems to treat the surrounding plebeians, now drawn into a tight circle around the body, as close friends. As a particularly dramatic touch, three of the conspirators—Casca, Cinna, and Decius Brutus—hover at the edge of the crowd, watching Antony's speech with increasing trepidation. As Antony's purpose becomes clear and the mob begins to take his side, they look at one another, come to a silent decision, and make their getaway.

The lynching of Cinna the Poet (III.iii) is omitted, or at least the dialogue is. His name appears in the cast list, and as the mob storms away from the Forum, tearing down market stalls and throwing things off stair landings, the camera passes swiftly by a body lying among the wreckage. Perhaps this is Cinna, efficiently done in.

The proscription scene (IV.i) is retained, as is the complexity of Antony's character. Antony and Octavius review their enemy list while enjoying a massage and steam bath; Lepidus, the third member of the triumvirate, stands by ready to run errands. Octavius is handsome, young, and self-confident; his rivalry with Antony is apparent, and one senses that Antony will eventually lose out.

In the quarrel scene between Brutus and Cassius (IV.iii), the actors can sustain a high level of intensity without becoming monotonous, since, thanks to the textual cuts, they do not have to sustain it very long. Richard Johnson's black-bearded, gloomy Cassius seems dangerous to the point of violence. He draws his dagger, but instead of obeying his momentary impulse to attack Brutus, he stabs it into a wooden table and invites Brutus to dispose of him (100–107). Jason Robards's Brutus is contrastingly fragile in physique, although immovably stubborn.

The battle scenes take place in a rocky and believable landscape, with numerous extras and plenty of horses. Brutus, who earlier saw Caesar's ghost by lamplight in his tent (IV.iii.275–286), is haunted during the battle by a double exposure vision of John Gielgud's reproachful face, whispering, "Et tu, Brute."

Besides considerable textual cutting in the last two acts, minor characters are combined or omitted. Titinius is present but does not kill himself. Brutus comes upon Cassius's body just before his own suicide. The closing lines, as in many other stage and screen productions, are rearranged so that Antony's is the final speech.

Among the additional touches that give the film a special resonance is the opening sequence, just before the credits. An eagle is wheeling about the sky, looking proudly imperial and symbolically Roman. Then we see that it is circling a battle-field. Skeletons of men and horses lie tangled with chariot wheels, and wildflow-ers bloom in the wreckage. A voice-over narrator tells us that this is the scene of Caesar's last battle, fought in Munda, Spain, against the sons of Pompey. The soundtrack then comes in with shouts of "Hail, Caesar," as the camera lingers on a grinning, helmeted skull and then segues into the play's opening scene, in which the Roman populace is gathering to celebrate this same victory. The sequence re-minds us of the violence and complexity of Caesar's life, as well as of the fact that he has just been involved in a civil war, Roman against Roman. His falling in death at the foot of the statue of Pompey, first his friend and then his enemy, gains in irony.

JULIUS CAESAR FOR TELEVISION, 1980

Between 1978 and 1985, the British Broadcasting Company, assisted by fund-ing from Time-Life and other sources, undertook the ambitious project of filming Shakespeare's entire canon. The BBC's policy was to present the full text of the plays to the extent possible. Each play was shown on British television and then public television stations in the United States.

Julius Caesar was directed by Herbert Wise and produced by Cedric Messina, with Charles Gray as Julius Caesar, Richard Pasco as Brutus, David Collings as Cassius, Keith Michell as Antony, Carrick Hagan as Octavius Caesar, Sam Dastor as Casca, Virginia McKenna as Portia, and Elizabeth Spriggs as Calphurnia. Cos-tumes were basically togas and tunics, and the locales were indoor studio sets.

The essentially uncut text has proved both a strength and a weakness. A major strength is the refreshing fact that scenes and characters ordinarily omitted, or se-verely shortened, are included. We have not only Cinna the Poet but the "camp poet" (IV.iii.123–138) who barges into Brutus's tent at Sardis. Young Cato appears at the battle of Philippi, vaunting his name (V.iv.4–6). Portia not only tells Brutus about cutting herself in the thigh but shows him the wound, a gory gash (II.i.299–301). A short time afterward, in a scene frequently cut in other produc-tions, Portia appears in the street with Lucius and encounters the Soothsayer (II.iii). Her nervous tension adds to the preassassination suspense and also fore-shadows her later suicide.

The production's weakness is that all of these scenes and speeches can get te-dious. The problem is not entirely in the no-cutting policy or in the consequent three-hour running time. The film's budget allowed neither spectacular sets nor agile camera work, resulting in what boils down to a procession of talking heads. Some variety is attempted; often we view a talking head over the shoulder of the person he is talking to, or we see two people conversing one behind the other, both facing the camera.

As if to compensate for the lack of spectacle, characterization has been thought-fully developed. Most of the actors are trained in Shakespeare and are accustomed to thinking through the implications of each line. Charles Gray's Julius Caesar is decidedly on the arrogant side, convinced that he is not like other men, and equipped with a jutting chin of the Mussolini-Caesar variety. Richard Pasco's Brutus speaks ponderously, hardly moving even his heavy-lidded eyes, while David Collings's Cassius jumps nervously about.

Keith Michell's Antony struck one critic as "too old and fleshy to be a vigorous and virile Antony."[58] Certainly he contrasts with the more muscular Antony of Brando and Heston. However, Michell is effective in his own way. His actions are more calculated, less spontaneous, and thus appropriate to the politically opportunistic side of Antony's multifaceted character. His power is that of a middle-aged man who has been successful so far at everything he has done, but who senses that his reserves of strength are not inexhaustible.

Antony thus supplies a foil for Garrick Hagan's young and inscrutable Octavius. The rivalry between these two is clearly drawn. In the final scene, Antony speaks his eulogy of Brutus, "This was the noblest Roman of them all" (V.v.68–75); Octavius, claiming the last lines as in Shakespeare's text, attempts to push Antony out of the spotlight by claiming Brutus's body: "Within my tent his bones tonight shall lie." Antony does have, however, if not the last line, the last shot; the camera lingers on him as he removes his cloak to cover Brutus's body.

Among the minor characters, Sam Dastor interprets Casca in a livelier fashion than is often the case. Instead of viewing events from a stance of deep personal boredom, as the text might suggest—"It [Antony's offer of a crown to Caesar] was mere foolery, I did not mark it" (I.ii.236)—this Casca is clearly delighted that Brutus and Cassius want to talk to him and pretends diffidence in order to lead them on to ask more. Being in the middle of the conspiracy energizes him. He bounces up and down, eyes alight. Whenever the crowd of conspirators confer, Casca edges as close as he can to the leaders. He is eager to be the first to stab Caesar, and he seems to assume that wonderful things will immediately begin to happen. When, instead, Antony enters (III.i.146) and Casca realizes that the future might hold some complications, his face falls, and he begins to edge out of the camera frame, away from Brutus and Cassius, and then out of the film entirely.

In the assassination scene itself, the camera's habit of coming very close to the action creates a bloody and confusing scene. One cannot tell whose dagger is hacking what. Perhaps the confusion is appropriate to the circumstances. The rhythm becomes contrastingly slow when Brutus, the last to strike, turns to Caesar, embraces him, and then stabs him with a dagger he has been holding behind his back.

The Forum scene (III.ii) includes a fairly large crowd of plebeians, relative to the size of the production, and the studio set creates some sense of space with rows of distant columns. Brutus gives a calm oration with studied gestures. Antony begins to speak, or to try to speak, through what appears to be a press of emotion. His calculation is visible to the audience, however. As the crowd loses its pro-Brutus fervor and begins to sympathize with Caesar, Antony watches their reactions, then whips them into a fervor. When Octavius's servant enters to announce his master's arrival, Antony is laughing with glee.

Surprisingly, since the production as a whole has so few textual cuts and since this scene does a good job of showing both Brutus's and Antony's effect on their hearers, the mob in the Forum has lost a few lines. Their admiring comments on Brutus— "Give him a statue with his ancestors," "Let him be Caesar" (III.ii.50–51)—have been omitted, with a certain loss of irony as Brutus claims, consciously at least, to eschew personal ambition. And at the end of Antony's speech, the mob makes no mention of burning anything, either Caesar's body or the conspirators' houses (253–257).

The lynching of Cinna the Poet, immediately following, is swift and somewhat confusing, partly because the camera is so close to the actors that faces seem to appear out of nowhere.

The proscription scene (IV.i) begins with a close-up of the list of victims to be killed. Antony is still self-confident, but his air of triumph has been mitigated by his rivalry with the stony-faced Octavius, and he comforts himself by pouring another cup of wine. Octavius foreshadows his straitlaced character in *Antony and Cleopatra* by declining a refill for himself.

After the quarrel between Brutus and Cassius (IV.iii), and the appearance of Caesar's ghost as a talking head in double exposure, the pace of the play slows even further. Act V drags its slow length along. The battle of Philippi is not shown on camera but is indicated by shouting on the soundtrack, a continuous roar, like a distant sporting event. Cassius's suicide is followed by that of Titinius, as in the text, and Brutus goes gloomily through his interminable search for someone to hold the sword for him to run upon. (Strato finally obliges.)

The film's small scale struck some critics as inappropriate. According to Robert E. Knoll, "This is not the Roman spectacle that the text seems to call for. . . . This is an *intimate* production of a *public* play."[59]

Susan Willis, however, points out some advantages of the close-up technique and also of the presentation of much of the dialogue as voice-over. "The close-ups, extreme close-ups, and voice-overs establish both style and interpretation in this tragedy of thought."[60] Brutus, Willis points out, has many voice-over thoughts before the assassination but then becomes "a man of speech during and after the deed, while the role of primary thinker shifts to Mark Antony, who has most of the voice-overs in the second half of the play. The icily calm Octavius, interestingly, has no voice-overs; we are left like Antony to guess at his thoughts."

On balance, the BBC's *Julius Caesar* might prove most valuable as a reference source, to be consulted for individual scenes rather than viewed as a whole and at one sitting. It lacks the dramatic sweep achieved consistently by the Mankiewicz version and occasionally by the Heston version. Yet through its attempt to do justice to the written text, it has created a unique production.

NOTES

1. John D. Ripley's *"Julius Caesar" on Stage in England and America, 1599–1973* (Cambridge: Cambridge University Press, 1980) is a thorough and scholarly survey of the

play's performance history to 1973. For listings of subsequent productions, see *World Shakespeare Bibliography*, brought out annually by *Shakespeare Quarterly*.

2. See J. R. Mulryne and Margaret Shewring, eds., *Shakespeare's Globe Rebuilt* (Cambridge: Cambridge University Press, 1997), a collection of essays on the scholarly investigations that have accompanied this project.

3. See Richard Covington, "The Rebirth of Shakespeare's Globe," *Smithsonian* 28 (November 1997), 64–76. The article includes color photographs made during the 1997 season.

4. Ronald Watkins and Jeremy Lemmon cite examples from *Julius Caesar* throughout their *In Shakespeare's Playhouse: The Poet's Method* (London: David and Charles, 1974).

5. T. W. Baldwin suggests that Caesar and Antony were played, respectively, by John Heminges and Henry Condell. *The Organization and Personnel of the Shakespearean Company* (New York: Russell and Russell, 1961), table II.

6. Richard and Helen Leacroft, in *Theatre and Playhouse: An Illustrated Survey of Theatre Building from Ancient Greece to the Present Day* (London: Methuen, 1984), give a panoramic yet detailed view of these developments.

7. Quoted by Ripley, *"Julius Caesar,"* p. 20, from "An Apology for the Life of Mr. Colley Cibber," ed. Robert W. Lowe, 1889. I have modernized the spelling and capitalization.

8. *Shakespeare's Julius Caesar, A Tragedy Adapted to the Stage by J. P. Kemble*, facsimile edited by John Ripley (London: Cornmarket Press, 1970). The Theatres Royal in London at the time included Covent Garden, Drury Lane, and the Haymarket.

9. See Eleanor Ruggles, *Prince of Players: Edwin Booth* (New York: Norton, 1953), pp. 3–60.

10. George C. D. Odell, *Annals of the New York Stage* (New York: AMS Press, 1937, repr. 1970), vol. 7, p. 639.

11. Ruggles, *Prince*, p. 166.

12. Timothy Hampton, *Writing from History: The Rhetoric of Exemplarity in Renaissance Literature* (Ithaca, N.Y.: Cornell University Press, 1990), p. 234.

13. Albert Furtwangler, *Assassin on Stage: Brutus, Hamlet, and the Death of Lincoln* (Urbana, Ill.: University of Illinois Press, 1992), p. 99–100.

14. Ruggles, *Prince*, p. 205, quotes the *New York Herald*.

15. Charles H. Shattuck, *Shakespeare on the American Stage: From the Hallams to Edwin Booth* (Washington, D.C.: Folger Shakespeare Library, 1976), pp. 146–147. For this quotation, Shattuck cites *The Season*, New York, December 30, 1871.

16. Booth's Theatre, on Twenty-third Street between Fifth and Sixth avenues, was to be demolished in the 1880s. The present Booth Theatre on Forty-fifth Street, a much smaller playhouse, opened in 1913.

17. Ripley, *"Julius Caesar,"* p. 116.

18. In *Pax Britannica: The Climax of an Empire* (New York: Harcourt Brace Jovanovich, 1968), James (later Jan) Morris vividly describes the Diamond Jubilee as it was celebrated around the globe. As the book's title implies, Morris finds frequent parallels between the British and the Roman empires.

19. Tree's original surname was Beerbohm. He adopted the name "Tree" early in his acting career and is sometimes referred to, and alphabetized, as "Beerbohm Tree," though without a hyphen. "Her Majesty's" was, and still is, the name of the theater. No special relationship with or sponsorship by the monarch is implied.

20. Quoted by Ralph Berry, "The Imperial Theme," in Richard Foulkes, ed., *Shakespeare and the Victorian Stage* (Cambridge: Cambridge University Press, 1986), p. 155.

21. Ibid., pp. 155, 156.

22. Ripley, "*Julius Caesar*," p. 163.

23. "From my heart I thank my beloved people," from a telegram sent by the queen to her dominions on the morning of June 22, 1897. Quoted by Morris, *Pax Britannica*, p. 21.

24. William Poel, founder in 1894 of the Elizabethan Stage Society, produced numerous Shakespeare plays but does not seem to have turned his attention at any length to *Julius Caesar*. Among those who did apply the new ideas to *Julius Caesar* were F. R. Benson, who emphasized rapid action, and William Bridges-Adams, who used close to a full text and thus restored much of the play's built-in ambiguity. For a detailed summary, see Ripley, "*Julius Caesar*," pp. 176–214.

25. John Houseman, *Run-Through: A Memoir* (New York: Simon & Schuster, 1972), pp. 298–299. Houseman gives a lively account of this production, including backstage gossip, the complexities of the company's funding, and the reactions of Welles's creative and hardworking associates when they discovered that Welles habitually took all the credit.

26. Ripley, "*Julius Caesar*," p. 223, cites Welles's comment from a bulletin put out by the Mercury Theatre, an organization Welles had founded and through which he presented *Julius Caesar*.

27. Houseman, *Run-Through*, p. 307.

28. *Time*, November 22, 1937, p. 43. I have regularized the spelling.

29. Richard France, ed., *Orson Welles on Shakespeare: The W.P.A. and Mercury Theatre Playscripts*, Contributions in Drama and Theatre Studies, no. 30 (Westport, Conn.: Greenwood Press, 1990), pp. 105–106. France cites a telephone interview with Lloyd in 1972.

30. *Time*, November 22, 1937, p. 43.

31. Ripley, "*Julius Caesar*," p. 268. This production was directed by Edward Payson Call.

32. This production was adapted by John Briggs and R. H. Deschamps and presented at the Florida Shakespeare Festival, Miami. See Peggy Goodman Endel, "*Julio Cesar* et al.; The 1986 Florida Shakespeare Festival," *SQ* 38 (1987), 214–216.

33. Cary Mazer, "Julius Caesar," *ShB* 6 (September/October–November/December 1988), pp. 32–33.

34. See Mary Beard, "Mixing It," *TLS*, August 13, 1993, p. 17. This production, directed by David Thacker, was staged at the Other Place, the Royal Shakespeare Company's small experimental theater in Stratford.

35. Langdon Brown, "*Julius Caesar*," in Samuel L. Leiter, ed., *Shakespeare Around the Globe: A Guide to Notable Postwar Productions* (Westport, Conn.: Greenwood Press, 1986), p. 278. The production was directed by Ron Daniels for the Royal Shakespeare Company. The video screen was removed later in the play's run.

36. Kenneth B. Steele, "*Julius Caesar*," *ShB* 8 (fall 1990), 12–13. The production was directed by Richard Monette and designed by Ultz.

37. Dorothy and Wayne Cook, "*Julius Caesar*," *ShB* 10 (spring 1992), 23–24. This production was directed by Steven Pimlott.

38. Dominique Goy-Blanquet, "Apolitical Aspects," *TLS*, April 17, 1987, p. 414.

39. Brown, in Leiter, pp. 274–275. The production was directed by John Schlesinger, with John Gielgud as Julius Caesar.

40. Beard, "Mixing It," p. 17.

41. Michael L. Greenwald, " 'An Enterprise of Great Pitch and Moment': *Julius Caesar* and *Antony and Cleopatra* at the Alley Theatre, 1996," *SQ* 48 (1997), 88.

42. Ripley, "*Julius Caesar*," p. 247. This production at the Shakespeare Memorial Theatre was directed by Antony Quayle and Michael Langham.

43. Ibid., p. 273. This production by the Royal Shakespeare Company was directed by Trevor Nunn.

44. Marjorie J. Oberlander, *"Julius Caesar," ShB* 6 (July–August 1988), 9. The production was directed by Stuart Vaughan.

45. Benedict Nightingale, in the *Times* of London, July 7, 1995, p. 35. The production was directed by Peter Hall for the Royal Shakespeare Company, Stratford-upon-Avon. The Rubicon, a small river, was the boundary between Italy proper and Cisalpine Gaul. By crossing it and entering Italy with his army, Caesar defied orders from the Senate and started the civil war against Pompey.

46. Ripley, *"Julius Caesar,"* p. 257.

47. Roy Walker, "Unto Caesar: A Review of Recent Productions," in William Rosen and Barbara Rosen, eds., *Julius Caesar* (New York: Signet, 1987), p. 220.

48. Kenneth Rothwell and Annabelle Henkin Melzer, *Shakespeare on Screen: An International Filmography and Videography* (New York: Neal-Schuman Publishers, 1990), pp. 112–126.

49. Jack J. Jorgens's *Shakespeare on Film* (Bloomington, Ind.: Indiana University Press, 1977) discusses the Mankiewicz *Julius Caesar* of 1953. Jo McMurtry's *Shakespeare Films in the Classroom: A Descriptive Guide* (Hamden, Conn.: Archon Books, 1994) deals with readily available films from the perspective of classroom teaching. *Shakespeare on Television: An Anthology of Essays and Reviews*, ed. J. C. Bulman and H. R. Coursen (Hanover, N.H.: University Press of New England, 1988) contains useful material on televised productions, as does Susan Willis's *The BBC Shakespeare Plays: Making the Televised Canon* (Chapel Hill, N.C.: University of North Carolina Press, 1991).

50. These include *Shakespeare Bulletin*, which since 1992 has incorporated the *Shakespeare on Film Newsletter*, *Shakespeare Quarterly*, *Shakespeare Newsletter*, and *Shakespeare and the Classroom*. Reviews of recent film releases may be found in many of the periodicals indexed in standard reference works, such as the *Readers Guide*. Periodicals devoted to film often include articles on Shakespearean films; among these are *Film Quarterly*, *Quarterly Review of Film and Video*, and *Sight and Sound*. *Literature/ Film Quarterly* occasionally publishes Shakespearean theme issues.

51. Jorgens, *Shakespeare on Film*, p. 319 n. 18. Jorgens quotes Ronald Hayman's *John Gielgud* (1971).

52. Ibid., p. 100 n. 12, p. 319.

53. Ibid., p. 100.

54. Ibid., p. 104.

55. Ibid., p. 96, cites Manvell, *Shakespeare and the Film* (New York: Praeger, 1971), pp. 86–87.

56. Robert F. Willson, Jr., "The Populist *Julius Caesar," ShB* 13 (summer 1995), 37–38.

57. Rothwell and Melzer, *Shakespeare on Screen*, p. 121. Rothwell quotes Thompson's review from the *New York Times*, February 4, 1971, p. 30.

58. Gerald Clarke, "Longest Run," *Time*, February 12, 1979, quoted in Bulman and Coursen, *Shakespeare on Television*, p. 250.

59. Robert E. Knoll, "The Shakespeare Plays: The First Season," *SFNL* 3 (April 1979), reprinted in Bulman and Coursen, *Shakespeare on Television*, p. 251.

60. Willis, *BBC Shakespeare Plays*, p. 198.

SELECTED ANNOTATED BIBLIOGRAPHY

This bibliography is designed to serve both readers who want to carry ideas from this book into further realms of exploration, and those who want to go back a few spaces, to fill in some background. In other words, both the expert and the beginner will find this list useful.

A large proportion of the works that appear in the chapter notes are included here. I have omitted some of those those that document incidental or fairly small-scale points. Conversely, I have included some items not cited in the chapters but helpful in getting one's feet on the Shakespearean ground, so to speak—for example, reference works and study guides. My annotation gives an idea of what a work is about, especially its relevance to *Julius Caesar*, but does not attempt to provide a complete abstract. Editions of *Julius Caesar* are not included here, since these are described in Chapter 1.

BIBLIOGRAPHIES, REFERENCE WORKS, AND STUDY GUIDES

Bergeron, David M., and Geraldo U. de Sousa. *Shakespeare: A Study and Research Guide.* 3rd ed., rev. Lawrence, Kan.: University Press of Kansas, 1995. Surveys resources in Shakespearean scholarship. Does not have a section specifically devoted to *Julius Caesar*, but many suggestions are relevant.

Bevington, David. *Shakespeare*. Goldentree Bibliographies in Language and Literature Series. Arlington Heights, Ill.: AHM Publishing Co., 1978. Useful information up to its publication date. Section on *Julius Caesar*.

Boyce, Charles. *Shakespeare A to Z: The Essential Reference to His Plays, His Poems, His Life and Times, and More*. New York: Roundtable Press, 1990. Quick reference with short articles. Especially good for individual characters in the plays.

Campbell, Oscar James. *The Reader's Encyclopedia of Shakespeare*. New York: Thomas Y. Crowell, 1966. Useful alphabetical reference with solid articles on Shakespearean scholarship and many individual scholars.

Champion, Larry S. *The Essential Shakespeare: An Annotated Bibliography of Major Modern Studies*. 2nd ed. New York: G. K. Hall, 1993. Detailed description of each item. Section on *Julius Caesar*.

McDonald, Russ. *The Bedford Companion to Shakespeare: An Introduction with Docu-ments*. Boston: Bedford Books of St. Martin's Press, 1996. Essays on backgrounds and sources, with excerpts from original documents. Many of the essays are relevant to *Julius Caesar*.

Scott, Mark W., ed. *Shakespearean Criticism: Excerpts from the Criticism of William Shakespeare's Plays and Poetry, from the First Published Appraisals to Current Evaluations*. Detroit, Mich.: Gale Research Co., 1988. Vol. 7, pp. 138–366, is the main section on *Julius Caesar*. For additional references, see the index in Vol. 23, as well as the supplements. Chronological arrangement. Excerpts are often lengthy and give the flavor as well as the argument of the piece.

Velz, John W. *Shakespeare and the Classical Tradition: A Critical Guide to Commentary, 1660–1960*. Minneapolis: University of Minnesota Press, 1968. A comprehensive listing for these three centuries, with summaries and annotations. Usefully indexed.

Wells, Stanley, ed. *The Cambridge Companion to Shakespeare Studies*. Cambridge: Cambridge University Press, 1986. Authoritative essays on many aspects of the field. Index leads to commentary on *Julius Caesar*.

———. *Shakespeare: A Bibliographical Guide*. Rev. ed. Oxford: Clarendon Press, 1990. Essays by various scholars. *Julius Caesar* is treated (with *Antony and Cleopatra*) by R.J.A. Weis, pp. 275–295.

ROMAN HISTORY AND LITERATURE, INCLUDING SHAKESPEARE'S SOURCES

Bowman, Alan K., Edward Champlin, and Andrew Lintott, eds. *The Cambridge Ancient History*. Vol. 10, *The Augustan Empire, 43 B.C.–A.D. 69*. 2nd ed. Cambridge: Cambridge University Press, 1982. Includes a description of the battle of Philippi.

Bullough, Geoffrey, ed. *Narrative and Dramatic Sources of Shakespeare*. Vol. 5, *The Roman Plays*. London: Routledge and Kegan Paul, 1964. For *Julius Caesar*, Bullough provides an introductory overview of the sources, followed by selections from Plutarch, Suetonius, Thomas Elyot's *The Governour*, the *Mirror for Magistrates*, Orlando Pescati's *Il Cesare*, the anonymous play *Caesar's Revenge*, and other possible influences. A useful sampling of the different ways Shakespeare's audience may have viewed the characters and events in the play.

Cook, S. A., F. E. Adcock, and M. P. Charlesworths, eds. *The Cambridge Ancient History*. Vol. 10, *The Augustan Empire, 44 B.C.–A.D. 70*. Cambridge: Cambridge University Press, 1934, 1952, 1966. This earlier edition provides a more detailed description of some of the events between the death of Caesar and the battle of Philippi.

Crook, J. A., Andrew Lintott, and Elizabeth Rawson. *The Cambridge Ancient History*. Vol. 9, *The Last Age of the Roman Republic, 146–43 B.C.* 2nd ed. Cambridge: Cambridge University Press, 1982. See especially Rawson, "The Aftermath of the Ides," pp. 468–490. Thorough documentation from original sources.

Dickinson, John. *Death of a Republic: Politics and Political Thought at Rome, 59–44 B.C.* New York: Macmillan, 1963. A historian's close-up view of the period.

Gelzer, Matthias. *Caesar: Politician and Statesman*. Trans. Peter Needham. Cambridge, Mass.: Harvard University Press, 1968. A scholarly biography of the historical Julius Caesar, scrupulously documented, emphasizing the political aspects of Caesar's life.

Grant, Michael. *Julius Caesar.* New York: M. Evans and Co., 1969, 1992. Describes personal as well as political aspects of Caesar, in the context of the ancient world.

MacCallum, M. W. *Shakespeare's Roman Plays and Their Background.* New York: St. Martin's, 1910, 1967. Emphasis on characters.

Marsh, Frank Burr. *A History of the Roman World from 146 to 30 B.C.* 3rd ed. London: Methuen, 1963. Useful historical context.

Rouse, W.H.D. *Shakespeare's Ovid, Being Arthur Golding's Translation of the Metamorphoses.* Carbondale, Ill.: Southern Illinois University Press, 1961. Based on Golding's 1567 edition. Original spelling.

Spencer, T.J.B. *Shakespeare's Plutarch.* Harmondsworth: Penguin, 1964. Thomas North's translation of the lives of Julius Caesar, Brutus, Antony, and Coriolanus. Modern spelling. Glossary.

Walter, Gerard. *Caesar: A Biography.* Trans. Emma Craufurd. New York: Scribner's, 1952. A vividly written biography of Julius Caesar, with some speculative description and dialogue.

PERFORMANCE ASPECTS

Baldwin, T. W. *The Organization and Personnel of the Shakespearean Company.* New York: Russell and Russell, 1961. Includes speculations, conjectural but interesting, on which actors originally played which parts.

Bentley, Gerald Eades. *The Profession of Player in Shakespeare's Time, 1590–1642.* Princeton, N.J.: Princeton University Press, 1984. Context for *Julius Caesar's* early performances.

Berry, Ralph. "The Imperial Theme." In Richard Foulkes, ed., *Shakespeare and the Victorian Stage*, pp. 153–160. Cambridge: Cambridge University Press, 1986. Discusses Herbert Beerbohm Tree's production of *Julius Caesar*, 1898.

Bulman, J. C., and H. R. Coursen. *Shakespeare on Television: An Anthology of Essays and Reviews.* Hanover, N.H.: University Press of New England, 1988. Includes material on several televised productions of *Julius Caesar*.

Chambers, E. K. *The Elizabethan Stage.* Oxford: Clarendon Press, 1923. Vol. 2 deals with the acting companies and the playhouses.

Cook, Ann Jennalie. *The Privileged Playgoers of Shakespeare's London, 1576–1642.* Princeton, N.J.: Princeton University Press, 1981. Argues for a higher level of education and sophistication in Shakespeare's audience than in the population as a whole.

France, Richard, ed. *Orson Welles on Shakespeare: The W.P.A. and Mercury Theatre Playscripts.* Contributions to Drama and Theatre Studies, no. 30. Westport, Conn.: Greenwood Press, 1990. For Welles's 1937 stage production of *Julius Caesar*, see pp. 103–168.

Furtwangler, Albert. *Assassin on Stage: Brutus, Hamlet, and the Death of Lincoln.* Urbana, Ill.: University of Illinois Press, 1992. Life and death of John Wilkes Booth, who had acted in *Julius Caesar* (as Antony) a few months before assassinating President Lincoln.

Gurr, Andrew. *Playgoing in Shakespeare's London.* Cambridge: Cambridge University Press, 1987. Discusses many aspects of the London theater scene from 1567 to 1642.

Houseman, John. *Run-Through: A Memoir.* New York: Simon & Schuster, 1972. A volume of Houseman's autobiography. Detailed description of the 1937 Orson Welles stage production of *Julius Caesar*.

Jorgens, Jack J. *Shakespeare on Film*. Bloomington, Ind.: Indiana University Press, 1977. Extensive discussion of the 1953 Mankiewicz film of *Julius Caesar*; pp. 92–105, 265–268, 318–320.

Kemble, John Philip. *Shakespeare's Julius Caesar: A Tragedy Adapted to the Stage*. London: Cornmarket Press, 1970. Facsimile of the acting edition published by Kemble in 1814. Edited and with an introduction by John D. Ripley. Textual cuts support Kemble's insistence on a balanced, heroic, and generally smoothed-out version of the play.

Leacroft, Richard, and Helen Leacroft. *Theatre and Playhouse: An Illustrated Survey of Theatre Building from Ancient Greece to the Present Day*. London: Methuen, 1984. Includes numerous theaters in which *Julius Caesar* has been performed.

Leiter, Samuel L., ed. *Shakespeare Around the Globe: A Guide to Notable Postwar Productions*. Westport, Conn.: Greenwood Press, 1986. Frequent entries on *Julius Caesar*.

McMurtry, Jo. *Shakespeare Films in the Classroom: A Descriptive Guide*. Hamden, Conn.: Archon Books, 1994. Discusses three films of *Julius Caesar* available on videotape (pp. 86–93).

Mullin, Donald. *Victorian Actors and Actresses in Review: A Dictionary of Contemporary Views of Representative British and American Actors and Actresses, 1837–1901*. Westport, Conn.: Greenwood Press, 1983. Excerpts from contemporary reviews. Index allows reader to specify a particular character (Brutus, say), then read about actors who played the role.

Mulryne, J. R., and Margaret Shewring, eds. *Shakespeare's Globe Rebuilt*. Cambridge: Cambridge University Press, 1997. Essays on the history of the reconstructed Globe Theatre in London, including archaeology and performance questions, with a selection of documents relating to Elizabethan playhouses. Demonstrates the energetic scholarship accompanying the Globe project.

Odell, George C. D. *Shakespeare from Betterton to Irving*. 2 vols. New York: Scribner's, 1930. Repr. Benjamin Blom, 1963. Compiled by a prolific theater historian, working in part from personal archives and memories. Index locates material on many productions of *Julius Caesar*.

Pearson, Hesketh. *Beerbohm Tree: His Life and Laughter*. New York: Harper and Brothers, 1956. For Beerbohm Tree's Shakespeare productions, especially *Julius Caesar*, see pp. 116–133.

Ripley, John D. *"Julius Caesar" on Stage in England and America, 1599–1973*. Cambridge: Cambridge University Press, 1980. Detailed and scholarly theater history. Indispensable for the period covered.

Rothwell, Kenneth S., and Annabelle H. Melzer. *Shakespeare on Screen: An International Filmography and Videography*. New York: Neal-Schuman Publishers, 1990. *Julius Caesar* section, pp. 112–126, comprises some forty items, with dates, casts, and descriptions.

Ruggles, Eleanor. *Prince of Players: Edwin Booth*. New York: Norton, 1953. Vividly written biography.

Shattuck, Charles H. *Shakespeare on the American Stage: From the Hallams to Edwin Booth*. Washington, D.C.: Folger Shakespeare Liberary, 1976. Frequent reference to productions of *Julius Caesar*.

————. *The Shakespeare Promptbooks: A Descriptive Catalogue*. Urbana, Ill.: University of Illinois Press, 1965. *Julius Caesar* prompt books are listed on pp. 172–191.

Watkins, Ronald, and Jeremy Lemmon. *In Shakespeare's Playhouse: The Poet's Method*. London: David and Charles, 1974. Frequent reference to *Julius Caesar* as the authors speculate on original performance techniques.

Williams, Clare, trans. *Thomas Platter's Travels in England, 1599*. London: Jonathan Cape, 1937. Williams translates the journal, originally written in German, and supplies a lengthy discussion of Platter's life and times. For Platter's description of a performance of *Julius Caesar* at the Globe, as well as such other London entertainments as cockfighting and bearbaiting, see pp. 166–170.

Willis, Susan. *The BBC Shakespeare Plays: Making the Televised Canon*. Chapel Hill, N.C.: University of North Carolina Press, 1991. Includes a discussion of the British Broadcasting Company's *Julius Caesar*, 1979.

SCHOLARSHIP AND CRITICISM

Bloom, Harold, ed. *William Shakespeare's Julius Caesar*. New York: Chelsea Publishers, 1988. Essays by various scholars.

Burckhardt, Sigurd. *Shakespearean Meanings*. Princeton, N.J.: Princeton University Press, 1968. See "How Not to Murder Caesar," pp. 3–21.

Burt, Richard A. "A Dangerous Rome: Shakespeare's *Julius Caesar* and the Discursive Determinism of Cultural Politics." In Marie-Rose Logan and Peter L. Rudnytsky, eds., *Contending Kingdoms: Historical, Psychological, and Feminist Approaches to the Literature of Sixteenth Century England and France*, pp. 109–127. Detroit, Mich.: Wayne State University Press, 1991. Contributes to the new historicist debate on subversive elements in the theater.

Charney, Maurice. *Shakespeare's Roman Plays: The Function of Imagery in the Drama*. Cambridge, Mass.: Harvard University Press, 1961. Special emphasis on fire imagery in *Julius Caesar*.

Cohen, Michael. "New Directions in Shakespeare Criticism." *ShN* 38 (Fall–Winter 1988), 28–29. Reports on a seminar held by the Folger Shakespeare Institute in 1988.

Dachslager, E. L. "The Most Unkindest Cut: A Note on *Julius Caesar*." *ELN* 11 (1973–1974), 258–259. Discusses Plutarch's description of Brutus wounding Caesar "in the privities."

Dean, Leonard F., ed. *Twentieth Century Interpretations of Julius Caesar: A Collection of Critical Essays*. Englewood Cliffs, N.J.: Prentice-Hall, 1968. Collection of essays by various scholars.

Drakakis, John. " 'Fashion It Thus': *Julius Caesar* and the Politics of Theatrical Representation." *ShS* 44 (1992), 65–73. Examines the subversive potential of theatrical representation in Elizabethan times.

Fergusson, Francis. *Trope and Allegory: Themes Common to Dante and Shakespeare*. Athens: University of Georgia Press, 1977. Finds no reason to assume Shakespeare read Dante.

Foakes, R. A. "An Approach to *Julius Caesar*." *SQ* 5 (1954), 259–270. Discusses problems implicit in identifying the subject of *Julius Caesar* and deciding if *Julius Caesar* is a unified work.

Fortin, René E. "*Julius Caesar*: An Experiment in Point of View." *SQ* 19 (1968), 341–347. Reviews comments on ambivalent responses to *Julius Caesar*; suggests the play's structure consists of varying subject-object relationships.

Freytag, Gustav. *Technique of the Drama: An Exposition of Dramatic Composition and Art*. Trans. Elias J. MacEwan. 2nd ed. Chicago: S. C. Griggs & Co., 1896. Repr. St. Clair Shores, Mich.: Scholarly Press, 1969.

Frye, Northrop. *Anatomy of Criticism: Four Essays*. Princeton, N.J.: Princeton University Press, 1957. An archetypal approach frequently of relevance to *Julius Caesar*, though Frye does not discuss this play at any length.

————. *Fools of Time: Studies in Shakespearean Tragedy*. Toronto: University of Toronto Press, 1967. Frequent mention of *Julius Caesar* in the context of Shakespeare's tragedies and histories.

Garber, Marjorie. *Dream in Shakespeare: From Metaphor to Metamorphosis*. New Haven, Conn.: Yale University Press, 1974. For dreams in *Julius Caesar*, see pp. 47–58.

Gerenday, Lynn de. "Play, Ritualization, and Ambivalence in *Julius Caesar*." *L&P* 24 (1974), 24–33. Describes the inner conflicts of Brutus.

Girard, René. *A Theatre of Envy: William Shakespeare*. Oxford: Oxford University Press, 1991. Discusses sacrifice and primitive ritual in *Julius Caesar*.

Goldberg, Jonathan. *James I and the Politics of Literature: Jonson, Shakespeare, Donne, and Their Contemporaries*. Baltimore: Johns Hopkins University Press, 1983. Mentions the king's approval of Julius Caesar (the historical figure).

Granville-Barker, Harley. *Prefaces to Shakespeare: Julius Caesar*. Portsmouth, N.H.: Heineman, 1995 (1925). The author's perspective is that of an actor and director.

Hampton, Timothy. *Writing from History: The Rhetoric of Exemplarity in Renaissance Literature*. Ithaca, N.Y.: Cornell University Press, 1990. Discusses Shakespeare, with references to *Julius Caesar*, pp. 198–236.

Herbert, Edward T. "Myth and Archetype in *Julius Caesar*." *Psychoanalytical Review* 57 (1970), 303–308. Relates *Julius Caesar* to patterns described by Freud.

Holland, Norman M. *Psychoanalysis and Shakespeare*. New York: McGraw-Hill, 1964; repr. Octagon Books, 1976. A comprehensive survey of criticism. *Julius Caesar* is mentioned throughout and specifically dealt with on pp. 212–214.

Honigmann, E.A.J. *Shakespeare: Seven Tragedies: The Dramatic Manipulation of Response*. New York: Harper & Row, 1976. Discusses *Julius Caesar*, with emphasis on Brutus, pp. 30–53.

Jones, Ernest. *Hamlet and Oedipus*. New York: Doubleday, 1949; repr. Norton, 1976. Discusses *Julius Caesar*, pp. 120–126.

Kahn, Coppélia. *Roman Shakespeare: Warriors, Wounds, and Women*. London: Routledge, 1997. Feminist perspective on *Julius Caesar* and other Shakespeare works.

Kaula, David. "Let Us Be Sacrificers: Religious Motifs in *Julius Caesar*." *ShStud* 14 (1981), 197–214. Analyzes religious and supernatural elements in the play.

Knight, G. Wilson. *The Imperial Theme: Further Interpretations of Shakespeare's Tragedies Including the Roman Plays*. London: Oxford University Press, 1931, 1939. *Julius Caesar* discussed pp. 32–95.

Leggatt, Alexander. *Shakespeare's Political Drama: The History Plays and the Roman Plays*. London: Routledge, 1988. Chapter on *Julius Caesar*, pp. 139–139. Focuses on characters.

Liebler, Naomi Conn. " 'Thou Bleeding Piece of Earth': The Ritual Ground of *Julius Caesar*." *ShStud* 14 (1981), 175–196. Discusses Shakespeare's knowledge of Roman religious festivals.

Marshall, Cynthia. "Portia's Wound, Calphurnia's Dream: Reading Character in *Julius Caesar*." *ELR* 24 (1994), 471–488. A feminist examination of these figures.

Miles, Geoffrey. *Shakespeare and the Constant Romans*. Oxford: Clarendon Press, 1996. *Julius Caesar* discussed pp. 123–148, with other references throughout. Emphasizes Senecan stoicism and Ciceronian decorum.

Miola, Robert. "Shakespeare and the Tyrannicide Debate." *RQ* 38 (1985), 271–289. Surveys opinions in Shakespeare's day on the morality of assassinating tyrants.

————. *Shakespeare's Rome*. Cambridge: Cambridge University Press, 1983. Analyzes *Julius Caesar* in terms of Roman history as seen by Shakespeare, pp. 76–115.

Miriam Joseph, Sister. *Shakespeare's Use of the Arts of Language*. New York: Hafner Publishing Company, 1947, 1966. References to *Julius Caesar* throughout. Antony's Forum speech (III.ii) analyzed, pp. 283–286.

Mooney, Michael E. " 'Passion, I See, Is Catching': The Rhetoric of *Julius Caesar*." *JEGP* 90 (1991), 31–50. Examines the relationship between the Roman mob and the audience in *Julius Caesar*.

Parker, Barbara L. "The Whore of Babylon and Shakespeare's *Julius Caesar*." *SEL* 35 (1995), 251–269. Feminist approach, including religious aspects.

Paster, Gail Kern. " 'In the Spirit of Men There Is No Blood': Blood as Trope of Gender in *Julius Caesar*." *SQ* 40 (1989), 284–298. Feminist perspective.

Rebhorn, Wayne A. "The Crisis of the Aristocracy in *Julius Caesar*." *RenQ* 43 (1990), 75–111. Parallels Shakespeare's Julius Caesar with the earl of Essex.

Reynolds, Robert C. "Ironic Epithet in *Julius Caesar*." *SQ* 24 (1973), 329–333. Builds on the ambiguities inherent in the play.

Rose, Mark. "Conjuring Caesar: Ceremony, History, and Authority in 1599." *ELR* 19 (1989), 291–304. *Julius Caesar* in the context of late sixteenth-century political and religious concerns.

Schanzer, Ernest. "*Julius Caesar* as a Problem Play." In Leonard F. Dean, ed., *Twentieth Century Interpretations of Julius Caesar*, pp. 67–72. Englewood Cliffs, N.J.: Prentice-Hall, 1968. Discusses the play's ambiguities.

Scragg, Leah. *Discovering Shakespeare's Meaning: An Introduction to the Study of Shakespeare's Dramatic Structures*. London: Longman, 1988. Discusses treatment of character in *Julius Caesar*, pp. 152–164.

Serpieri, Alessandro. "Reading the Signs: Towards a Semiotics of Shakespearean Drama." Trans. Keir Elam. In John Drakakis, ed., *Alternative Shakespeares*, pp. 119–143. London: Methuen, 1985. Deals with *Julius Caesar* and *Othello*.

Smith, Bruce R. *Homosexual Desire in Shakespeare's England: A Cultural Poetics*. Chicago: University of Chicago Press, 1991. Discusses the society of same-sex friendship described by Plutarch, p. 277.

Smith, Gordon Ross. "Brutus, Virtue, and Will." *SQ* 10 (1959), 367–379. Includes a psychoanalytical reading.

Smith, Warren D. "The Duplicate Revelation of Portia's Death." *SQ* 4 (1953), 153–161. On a textual crux in *Julius Caesar*, IV.iii.

Sprengnether, Madelon. "Annihilating Intimacy in *Coriolanus*." In Mary Beth Rose, ed., *Women in the Middle Ages and the Renaissance: Literary and Historical Perspectives*. Syracuse, N.Y.: Syracuse University Press, 1986. Comments on Portia in *Julius Caesar*, p. 96.

Stirling, Brents. "*Julius Caesar* in Revision." *SQ* 13 (1962), 187–205. Part of the critical debate on the textual crux of IV.iii.

Tillyard, E.M.W. *The Elizabethan World Picture*. London: Chatto and Windus, 1943. Sees political and poetic patterns in the Renaissance as following an ideal of harmonious hierarchy. In recent years, this view has been accused of oversimplification.

Trousdale, Marion. *Shakespeare and the Rhetoricians*. Chapel Hill, N.C.: University of North Carolina Press, 1982. Discussion of Shakespeare's use of rhetoric is of general relevance to *Julius Caesar*, although the play itself is not treated in detail.

Ure, Peter, ed. *Shakespeare: Julius Caesar*. Casebook Series. London: Macmillan, 1969.
    Reprints articles and excerpts from early times through the 1960s.
Velz, John W. "Clemency, Will, and Just Cause in *Julius Caesar*." *ShS* 22 (1969), 109–118.
    Relates one of *Julius Caesar*'s textual cruxes (III.i.47-48) to a passage in Seneca.
———. "Undular Structure in *Julius Caesar*." *MLR* 66 (1971), 21–30. Elucidates the ris-
    ing and falling pattern in *Julius Caesar*'s plot.
Wilson, Richard. *Julius Caesar*. Penguin Critical Studies. London: Penguin, 1992. A new
    historicist approach.

INDEX

Names of characters in *Julius Caesar* appear in **bold type**.

About the Author

JO McMURTRY is Professor of English at the University of Richmond. She has published widely on Shakespeare, and her most recent books include *Shakespeare Films in the Classroom: A Descriptive Guide* (1994), and *Understanding Shakespeare's England: A Companion for the American Reader* (1989).

ISBN 0-313-30479-3

90000>

EAN

9 780313 304798

HARDCOVER BAR CODE